HURGHA[

DIVING GUIDE

SWAN·HILL
PRESS

HURGHADA

DIVING GUIDE

TEXT AND PHOTOGRAPHS
Massimo Bicciato
Giorgio Mesturini

DRAWINGS THE DIVES AND THE MAPS
Domitilla Müller

GRAPHIC DESIGN
Elena Tomasino

TRANSLATION
C.T.M., Milan

© 2001 White Star S.r.l.
Via Candido Sassone, 24 - Vercelli, Italy.

First Published in the UK in 2001
by Swan Hill Press, an imprint of Airlife
Publishing Ltd.

British Library Cataloguing-in-Publication Data
A catalogue record for this book
is available from the British Library

ISBN 1 84037 292 3

The information in this book is true and complete to the best
of our knowledge. All recommendations are made without
any guarantee on the part of the Publisher, who also disclaims
any liability incurred in connection with the use of this data
or specific details.

All rights reserved. No part of this book may be reproduced
or transmitted in any form or by any means, electronic or
mechanical including photocopying, recording or by any
information storage and retrieval system, without permission
from the Publisher in writing.

Printed in Italy

SWAN HILL PRESS
an imprint of Airlife Publishing Ltd.
101 Longden Road, Shrewsbury
SY3 9EB, England
E-mail: airlife@airlifebooks.com
Website: www.airlifebooks.com

CONTENTS

1 Alcyonarians and sponges in a thousand colors are features of Hurghada's waters.

2-3 Coral beaches and semi-emerged reefs: this is Hurghada for visitors in search of underwater sensations.

A - A school of blackspotted sweetlips (Plectorhinchus gaterinus) circles near the coral seabed in search of small invertebrates and crustaceans.

B – A group of bottlenose dolphins, typically gray with a slightly darker back, deftly cross the boat's wake.

C – Gaudy red and yellow alcyonarians, or soft corals, are quite common in the Red Sea.

D – With its treacherous reefs, the Straits of Gobal has always been a fearsome passage for boats crossing the Red Sea.

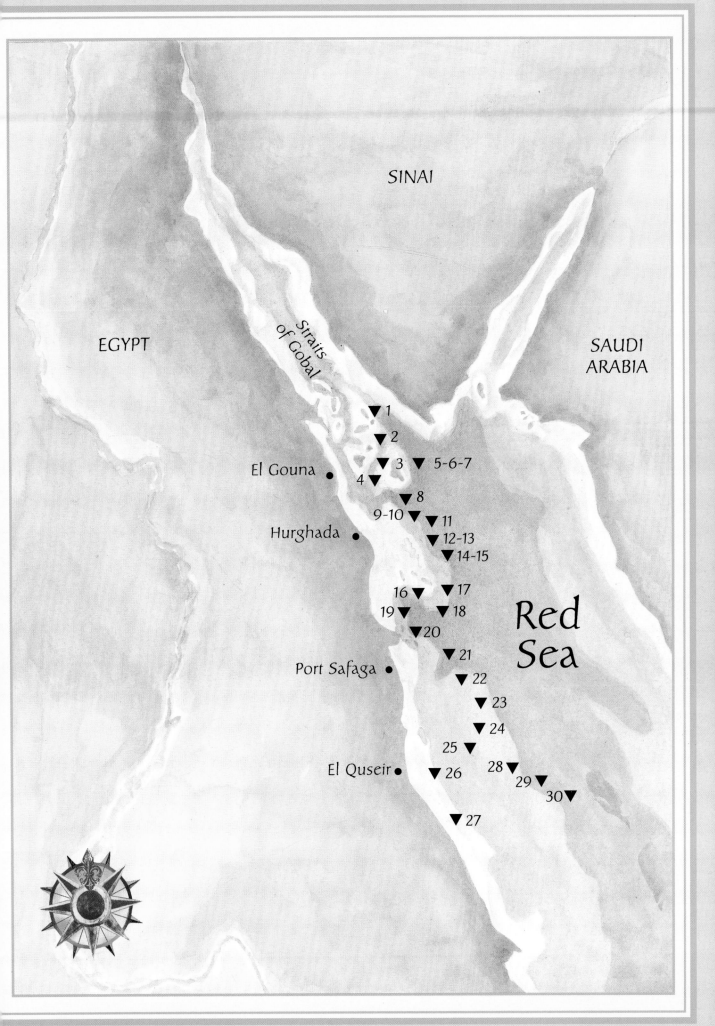

SINAI

EGYPT

SAUDI
ARABIA

Straits
of Gobal

▼ 1

▼ 2

El Gouna ● ▼ 3 ▼ 5-6-7

4 ▼

▼ 8

9-10 ▼ ▼ 11

Hurghada ● ▼ 12-13

▼ 14-15

16 ▼ ▼ 17

19 ▼ ▼ 18

▼ 20

▼ 21

Port Safaga ● ▼ 22

▼ 23

▼ 24

25 ▼

El Quseir ● ▼ 26 28 ▼

29 ▼

30 ▼

▼ 27

Red
Sea

Introduction

OBSERVING THE RED SEA from satellite images, we can see a narrow, elongated blue tongue that separates the African coast from the Arabian Peninsula. The Red Sea runs for 2200 kilometers from the Gulf of Suez in the north to the Straits of Bab el-Mandab, reaching a maximum width of 350 kilometers between the coasts of Eritrea and Saudi Arabia. In the north, it separates into two branches, separated by the mountainous Sinai massif. The western arm forms the Gulf of Suez with its deep inlets, while the eastern arm creates the Gulf of Aqaba, which is narrow and short yet hides depths in excess of 1600 meters. The reason it is so deep is the break between the Asiatic and African continental plates that runs from the Dead Sea, crosses the Gulf of Aqaba, and continues down the middle of the Red Sea, forming a clear break between the two continents, where the water may be over 2500 meters deep.

The Red Sea is a continuously evolving body of water, the still incomplete result of a process that began over 70 million years ago, when a portion of the ancient Mediterranean, the Tethys Sea, overflowed this territory. The first transformation took place about 20 million years ago, when the Red Sea

A

A – This photo clearly shows the two northern arms of the Red Sea, separated by the Sinai Peninsula. Inland, the course of the Nile is visible along the western coast of Egypt.

B – A satellite image of the entire Red Sea basin, comprised, to the north, of the western arm of the Gulf of Suez and the eastern arm of the Gulf of Aqaba, while to the south the entry to the Indian Ocean from the Straits of di Bab el-Mandeb can clearly be seen.

was cut off from the Indian Ocean and joined the Mediterranean through a narrow channel. It reached its current conformation when further shifts in the continental plates completely obstructed the connection with the Mediterranean, but opened a southern passage to the Indian Ocean, now known as the Straits of Bab el-Mandeb.

The Red Sea still has not yet reached its final conformation. Recent studies have shown that the Arabian and Egyptian shores are constantly shifting, moving away from each other at the rate of about two centimeters a year.

Beginning with this unique, constantly evolving geological situation, some researchers have hypothesized that in the future this narrow sea could open up to create an immense ocean.

The morphological origin of the Red Sea is quite complex. Various theories have been advanced to explain the link between the color red and the name of the sea. As early as Roman times, it was called "Mare Erythraeum," a word with Greek origins that means "red," from *erythròs*. Another theory comes from the custom of Greek sailors to associate a color with each cardinal direction, so that black, which emotionally inspires feelings of dark and cold, was used to indicate the north (it's no coincidence that the Black Sea is located north of Greece). Red, the symbol of fire, heat and sun, was instead associated with the south, and in fact the Red Sea is located to the south of the Hellenic peninsula.

But the question is still open. Some researchers feel that the name has a biological and not historical origin, derived from the presence of massive amounts of the planktonic algae *Trichodesmium erythraeum*, which during certain times of the year create a reddish mucilage on the surface of the sea.

The fish that inhabit these waters are in many ways similar to those in the Indian Ocean. This sea, squeezed between two continents, has only the Straits of Bab el-Mandeb as a natural opening for the exchange of waters; the result is that over the course of evolution, 17% of its fish species have remained endemic – that is, these species live only in these waters. The reefs are a complex ecosystem formed of various stony coral species that create an intricate tangle of corals, providing a home for most of the vast array of creatures that populate the waters of "Bahar el Ahmar" (the Arabic name for the Red Sea). This sea's spectacular coral reef enjoys undisputed fame with divers all over the world.

A

Environmental protection

B

A - This aerial view shows the reefs of the Hurghada archipelago, an immense coral maze that runs as far as the Straits of Gobal.

B - The northern side of the island of Zabargad. The island's geological composition is clear: the darker area is the volcanic zone of origin.

C – These sea swallows were photographed on Rocky Island. During the summer months countless swallows arrive to lay their eggs.

D - The Sabre squirrelfish (Sargocentron spiniferum), commonly known as the squirrelfish, has a flat, robust body with rosy tones. The preoperculate fin can cause painful injuries.

THE CORAL REEF is a particularly delicate, vulnerable ecosystem. All it takes are minimal changes in the sea's chemical factors or climate conditions to cause serious changes in the reef habitat.

For years, the Red Sea has been one of the most famous and popular exotic travel destinations, but now, unfortunately, we have begun to see the damage caused by increasingly invasive tourism encroaching on this fragile ecosystem. Irreparable changes have not yet occurred, but the sharp increase in tourism should be accompanied by provisions to protect the marine environment. The divers who daily plunge into these waters should know that any blow of their flippers could break the extremely fragile coral branches, which could then require over a decade to return to their original appearance.

Fortunately, in recent years some governments of countries bordering the Red Sea have become aware of its enormous tourism potential and have recognized the need to protect the marine environment by creating a number of protected areas.

The Egyptian government was the first to promote a policy of environmental protection. In 1983, it opened a land and marine national park on the islands of Tiran and Sanafir in the Ras Mohammed territories in the Sinai, to protect all these areas from the sharp increase in tourism.

Subsequently, again along the eastern coasts of the Sinai region, two other protected areas were created: Nabq, a few kilometers north of Naama Bay, and Ras Abu Galum, between the town of Dahab and Nuweiba. These two vast areas, located near a coast full of luxuriant plant life formed of dense mangroves, is an ideal habitat for many animals, especially birds, many of whom nest here. It also offers a wealth of marine creatures who find refuge among the roots of the trees.

E – In marvelous maneuvers, a school of striped dolphins lets itself be carried in the wake of the bow.

F – The absolute transparency of the water is amazing, set off by the fantastic colors of the corals that create the reefs of the Red Sea.

G – Fire coral (Millepora dichotoma), identifiable by its pale yellow fans, can cause severe burns if it comes in contact with the skin.

H – Before going to sleep, the parrotfish (Cetoscarus bicolor) creates a sort of protective cocoon around itself that seals in its odor, thus preventing it from being identified by predators.

The great impact tourism had on Hurghada beginning in the early 1990s created serious consequences for the marine ecosystem. In 1992, this resulted in the foundation of HEPCA, the Hurghada Environmental Protection and Conservation Association, a non-governmental but officially recognized organization that actively works to protect the underwater environment in the Egyptian Red Sea. Through donations and private initiatives, over the years HEPCA has collected the funds necessary to implement various projects, such as placing numerous mooring buoys near the reefs, thus reducing the damage once caused when anchors were cast onto the coral reefs.

The Red Sea Marine Park was created in 1998, when the law protecting the marine environment went into effect. It also protects the immense natural heritage of Brothers Islands, Daedalus Reef, Zabargad and Rocky Island.

Tourist cruise boats, which allow divers to reach these islands, must also follow strict environmental regulations to avoid altering the delicate balance that nature has achieved in these lonely stretches of sea.

In addition, through its cultural and informational activities, HEPCA promotes important initiatives concerning the Red Sea's environmental problems. Its goal is to convey a clear message of protection aimed not only at tourists, but especially operators, diving guides, and local residents, to make them aware of the fact that nature and environmental

conservation are the true driving forces of these magnificent places. The existence of the Marine Park and complete dedication to this task of creating awareness, give us reason for optimism when we look to the future of this sea, which needs increasingly close protection.

Underwater photography

WITH THE WEALTH of its waters, the Red Sea has always been an ideal place for underwater photography. Indeed, the coral reefs of Egypt and the Sudan attracted the attention of the very first people to document the underwater world. As early as 1949, a young Hans Hass took photos of the Sudanese waters and created the feature film *Adventure in the Red Sea*, which helped create new interest in underwater biological research. Following this, in 1952 Bruno Vailati organized an Italian expedition to shoot the film *Sesto Continente*, with the participation of a young Folco Quilici.

The Red Sea then became the setting for the enterprises of Captain Jacques Cousteau, whose first expedition to Sudanese waters took place in December 1951. His plan was to design an underwater village where a group of experts would live for a month, in constant contact with underwater life. During the expedition, known as "Precontinent II," he made the Oscar-winning film *World Without Sun*.

The fact that these diving pioneers found their best subject matter in these waters is certainly no coincidence. Their films and photography inspired entire generations of enthusiasts and are still testimony to the power of luxuriant coral growth in this sea.

The Red Sea is ideal for anyone who loves underwater photography, both because of the transparency of its waters, with visibility often over 30 meters, and the biological wealth of coral life, which vaunts an extraordinary variety of underwater flora and fauna. There is no need for deep dives or sophisticated equipment to find interesting subjects that offer good results. In fact, you can take interesting, unusual shots even just a few meters down, where the waves crash onto the reef and sunlight completely illuminates the shallow seabed.

To be able to take the most beautiful, evocative pictures in the

A – An underwater photographer enters the water. This is an important time to secure your equipment to avoid any accidental bumps.

B – Various models of waterproof cases can be used to bring video cameras underwater to film special details of underwater life. A photographer cautiously approaches a school of dolphins, who curiously allow themselves to be filmed.

C optical system, ideal for those who want to take photos without going too deep (they may not be watertight under great pressure), to more versatile equipment, such as watertight cameras with interchangeable lenses, to waterproof cases that can hold photographic equipment for outside use.

Camera equipment is only as good as the lighting. You need at least one flash that will provide enough illumination to create a faithful reproduction of the gorgeous colors of the marine world.

You should also remember that to take good underwater photos, good equipment and great technical knowledge are not enough. What is indispensable is to be at your ease in the water, thus allowing you to approach your subjects more easily.

Red Sea, you need some knowledge of the biological environment. That is, you need to know how to seek out and find a potential subject in as precise and careful a manner as possible.

While for years underwater photography was considered something for professionals only, today it's quite popular with amateurs as well, ordinary divers who simply want to take a few photos during their excursions.

Equipment for underwater photography has been designed to meet both strategic and scientific needs. The first underwater cameras, created by Hans Hass, made way for the famous "Calypso," the first fully underwater camera with watertight seals, created by Cousteau's team.

Since then, development has continued at a steady pace, although some models still on the market (Nikonos) are nothing more than perfected offshoots of the old "Calypso."

Today, the market offers endless possibilities for every need: from watertight cameras with a fixed

C – A photographer is concentrating on a close-up shot. For best results in underwater photography, maintain a good position in the water that provides maximum stability.

D – A humphead wrasse circles in the blue depths, posing for the photographer: don't be deceived by its brilliant green color, which requires a slight overexposure for a proper final exposure.

Straits of Gobal

O N MAPS, THE STRETCH OF SEA between the islands of Gobal, Shadwan, and the west coast of the southern Sinai is called the Straits of Gobal.

This area, which is the southern extension of the Gulf of Suez, has always been a feared passage for boats crossing the Red Sea, due to its menacing reefs that have caused numerous shipwrecks in the past. Since ancient times, the waters of the Red Sea, like those of the Mediterranean, have been one of the primary means of communication among the various civilizations that during different epochs settled along the coasts of North Africa, the Middle East and Europe.

With the opening of the Suez Canal on September 17, 1869, naval traffic increased considerably. At first, the primary users of this new route were ships in the British fleet, constantly in contact with colonies in the Indian Ocean. Through the British admiralty, in the early 1900s a group of lighthouses was built to make the ships' routes safer. Proof of how dangerous navigation in this part of the sea was can be seen by diving near the reef of Abu Nuhas, with its row of four shipwrecks dating from the late 1800s to modern times. Other sunken ships can be found near Gobal Island as well. Shipwreck sites are generally battered by large waves, so on days when the wind is strong it is often impossible to dive.

This area has more shipwrecks than anywhere else in the Egyptian Red Sea.

Despite much research, we still don't know exactly how many shipwrecks there are in the Red Sea. Information on the exact dates and causes of wrecks is still confusing and uncertain for many vessels.

Some of these ships, resting among the corals for decades now, have transformed into extraordinary containers of life and have become a safe refuge for various communities of fish.

Many of these wrecks still have their internal furnishings and original cargo. Don't succumb to the temptation to take same mementos from the ship. Instead, let other visitors see and enjoy this testimony so fundamental to the history of Red Sea navigation.

The Straits of Gobal offer more than mysterious, fascinating shipwrecks. This part of the sea contains numerous

A – An old, abandoned signal light stands guard on Tawila Island. All the old oil lighthouses have been gradually replaced by modern solar-powered lights.

B – The bow of a ship that foundered on the reef of Abu Nuhas is testimony to the danger of these waters, where the semi-emerged reef leaves no room for even the slightest error in course.

C – Small Gobal Island is entirely surrounded by a rich coral reef that extends toward the open sea. The transparent waters reveal a myriad of stony coral formations.

D – Traditional fishing boats with circular nets ply the outer reefs. Fishermen often run the risk of being stung by poisonous fish.

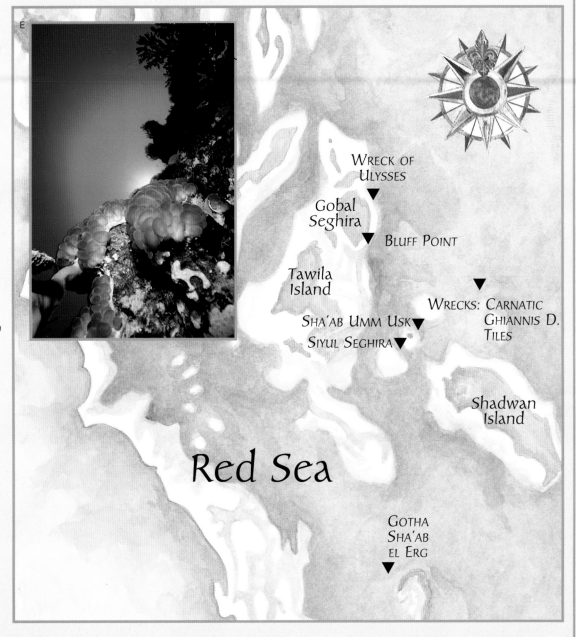

WRECK OF ULYSSES ▼

Gobal Seghira

▼ BLUFF POINT

Tawila Island

SHA'AB UMM USK ▼

SIYUL SEGHIRA ▼

▼ WRECKS: CARNATIC GHIANNIS D. TILES

Shadwan Island

Red Sea

GOTHA SHA'AB EL ERG ▼

reefs with extremely diverse forms and environments, all of which are quite interesting. You'll encounter larger pelagic species like sharks, tunas, barracudas, mantas, and pods of dolphins, a constant presence in the waters around several coral reefs, including Sha'ab el Erg and Umm Usk.

The best way to dive on the wrecks or admire the solitary reefs of Gobal is through cruise ships. The great advantage that a diving cruise offers is that you can dive around coral reefs far from the usual itineraries of day trips, in areas where the waters are still

virgin and pristine. Diving areas where "daily boats" travel every day are different and more interesting if explored during a cruise, as you'll have the opportunity to dive at the best times and avoid the masses of boats on daily diving trips. Red Sea cruises are usually one to two weeks long, with routes and itineraries designed to reach very exclusive destinations, such as shipwrecks or reefs in the Straits of Gobal, lonely Brothers Islands off the coast of Quseir, and the most unexplored areas of the southern Red Sea bordering Sudan.

E – The grape coral (Plerogyra sinuosa) consists of a mass of bladders in the classic form of a bunch of grapes, and may reach 80 centimeters in diameter.

F – The coast of Gobal Island consists of calcareous fossils of ancient coral reefs - a succession of inlets with small hidden beaches that offer shelter to crabs, mollusks and colonies of sea swallows.

Wreck of Ulysses

THIS ENGLISH MERCHANT SHIP, 90 meters long with a tonnage of 1900 tons, was built in Newcastle by Andrew Leslie & Co. and launched under the name *Diomed* in 1871.

It had bad luck from the start, and after a few months of navigation it foundered right in the Red Sea without suffering great damage. Unfortunately, the bad luck continued until, through unpardonable negligence by Captain Bremner, early in the morning of August 16, 1887, the *Ulysses* sank while traveling from the Suez Canal to the port of Penang, India. Convinced he could pass the coast of the island of Gobal Seghir on the west side, the ship ran fatally aground. It was probably the poor nautical maps that ships had in the late 1800s and the strong north winds that caused the

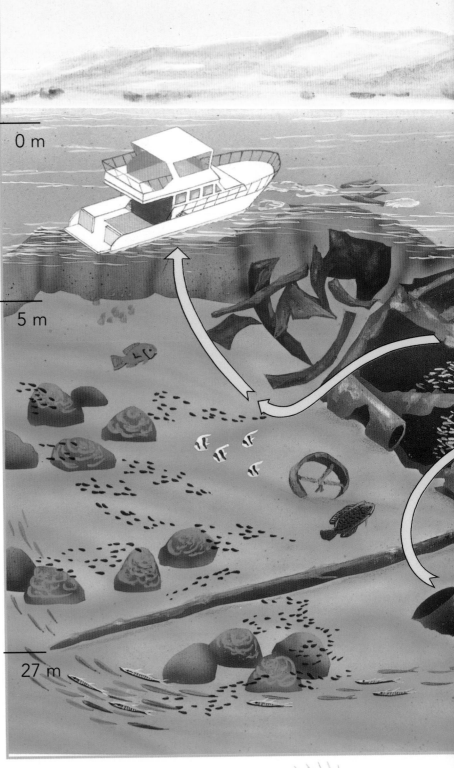

0 m

5 m

27 m

Ulysses to strike Gobal Island's large reef. As it lies near a very windswept reef, the ship cannot always be explored due to the strong currents that violently batter the north side of the reef. During its tremendous impact against the coral reef, the ship broke into two pieces and sank immediately. Today, as you descend along this reef, you'll see the remains of the prow of the *Ulysses* resting along the wall of Gobal, just five

A – The remains of the first class deck of the wreck of the Ulysses: a maze of metallic structures filtered by the rays of the sun, creating splendid patterns of light and shadow.

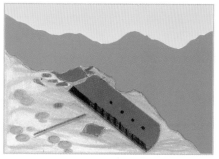

N

Gobal Seghira

WRECK
OF ULYSSES

▼

● BLUFF POINT

Tawila Island

Continuing your exploration along the upper deck, you can see the completely empty hold and the remains of the mainmast, encrusted and resting on the coral floor next to the hull.

Halfway up the ship, a large crack leads into the interior, where, with the aid of a flashlight, you can discover the

various sectors of the engine room.

Scattered on the floor around the wreck, you can see some of the remains of the hull, the ship's cargo and the gigantic smokestack, which was strewn across the surrounding area upon impact with the reef. On its last voyage, the *Ulysses* was carrying various types of electrical material. In fact, you can now find ceramic insulation, cables and other electrical equipment encrusted with coral.

meters below the surface, while the back two thirds of the ship lying on the floor below, 27 meters deep. More than a century after it foundered, the structures of the wreck are quite decayed and full of cracks, which have become convenient passageways to the now completely empty hold.

Start your dive from the stern. You can see the ship resting on the port side, where the enormous rudder and large propeller are visible, with a few blades resting partially submerged under the sandy floor.

The area below the stern is a comfortable hiding place for a large grouper and various crocodilefish, which are easily visible on the sand in the shelter of the propeller blades.

A – The reef will gradually encompass all the structures of the Ulysses. Even now, some parts of the wreck are hard to identify: an enormous iron wheel has now become an integral part of the reef.

B – The bulkhead frames are the skeleton of the ship, and the light that penetrates from the surface gives a ghostly appearance to the empty holds.

C – A typical late 19th century bathtub, which presumably fell out of the command cabin, is now lying on the bottom of the sea. Over the years, the corals have encrusted a large part of the ship's cargo.

D – Dense schools of glassfish find refuge from predators by taking shelter within the dark holds of the ship, which lies imposing and silent on the reef of the island of Gobal Seghira.

E – The wreck of the Ulysses lies on its left side, with corals now in full possession of it. The metal parts offer a stable support for the growth of stony corals.

F – The bulkhead frames are now welded to the coral floor a few meters deep. Upon impact with the reef, one third of the ship's bow was pulled off, and now lies on the reef.

E

F

Especially striking is a large metal wheel with spokes, partially buried in the sand halfway up the wreck, which makes an excellent subject for photography.

When you finish your exploration, return up following the ship's bulwarks until you reach the remains of the bow area, scattered on the reef at a depth of five meters. Here, the reef is strewn with wreckage the waves have scattered along the reef, and is now completely covered by a multitude of colorful organisms. The anchor chain lowered from the hawsehole can be seen encrusted in the coral wall.

A cloud of Indo-Pacific sergeant majors (*Abudefduf vaigiensis*), anthias, small groupers, and many other coral fish surround the bow of the ship. Due to the luminous underwater environment, it offers photographers a chance to take truly spectacular shots of this old steamer.

Bluff Point

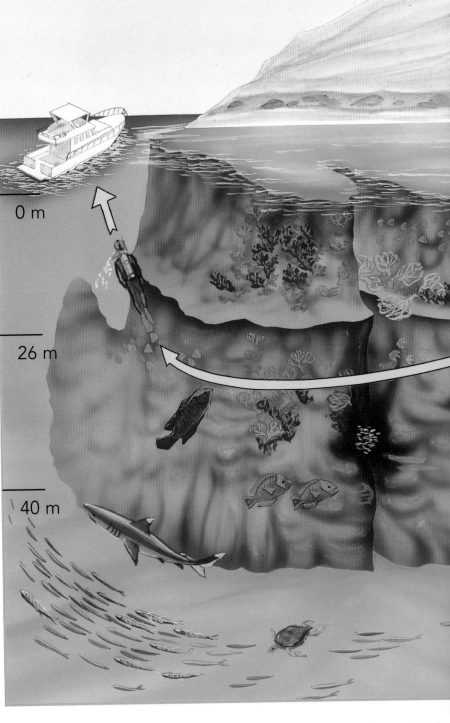

O N THE WESTERN SIDE of the Gobal Canal, north of Abu Nuhas reef, are the islands of Gobal Seghira and Gobal Kebira, connected by a narrow isthmus of sand.

On the southeast side of Gobal Seghira, the smallest of the two islands, is a massive promontory known as Bluff Point. You can recognize it by its small, yet vitally important lighthouse that permits ships in transit to follow the center of the canal and avoid perilous reefs like Abu Nuhas, which has caused countless shipwrecks.

Your dive can follow two distinct itineraries, which you can choose depending on the direction and force of the current, which can be quite powerful in this area.

On calm days, jump in from the boat

0 m

26 m

40 m

A

B

A – Striped dolphins are very common in the Red Sea. They live in pods consisting of no more than 15-20 individuals, and are grayish in color in the dorsal area with a light ventral area.

B – A large green turtle (Chelonia mydas) swims along the Gobal Seghira reef. These turtles are quite common, as they use the island's beach to deposit their eggs.

moored in the lagoon southwest of Bluff Point. Keeping the reef to your left, follow this especially spectacular wall that plunges over 40 meters, full of coral formations, gorgonians and terraces. Water transparency in this area is affected by the northeast wind, which can carry suspended waters toward the coast, thus reducing visibility.

Carefully observing the floor, at about 40 meters you will see massive

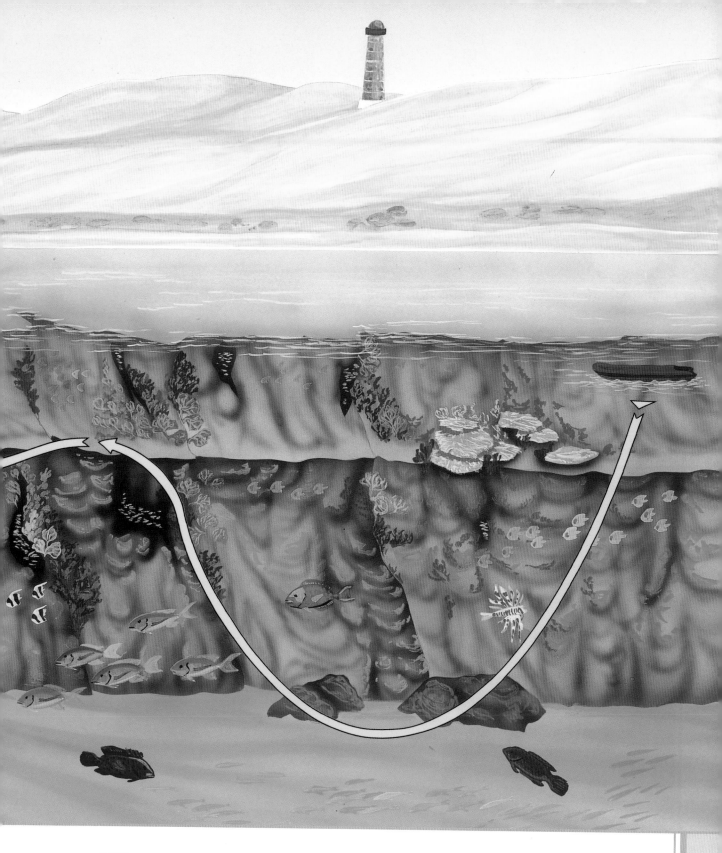

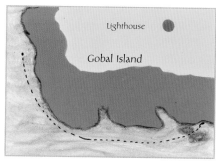

The lonely, tranquil beaches that run along the coast of the Gobal Islands are an ideal place for turtles to deposit their eggs. During the summer months, it's common to see various types of sea turtles, such as *Eretmochelys imbricata* or *Chelonia mydas*, as they swim along the walls of the reef.

The second itinerary is a drift dive. Take a raft to the east side of Bluff Point, then follow the current along the entire promontory, keeping the wall of the reef on your right. The best time to admire the colors of the wall is mid-morning, when the sunlight completely illuminates the east wall. While the current gently pushes you toward the boat's mooring point, watch for possible unexpected encounters from the blue depths. It's not uncommon to run into whitetip reef sharks (*Triaenodon obesus*), tunas, or even pods of bottlenose dolphins.

Little is known about the small barge lying at a depth of 12 meters below the boat mooring area. It was probably used to supply water to people who once worked on the island. The small wreck is especially interesting to visit at night, when your flashlight will illuminate the wreckage of the hull, revealing a myriad of nocturnal creatures who take advantage of the dark to abandon the crevices in which they take refuge during the day. You can admire multi-hued crinoids, *Astroba nuda* starfish, and steephead parrotfish (*Scarus gibbus*), who sleep among the corals wrapped in their characteristic bubbles of mucus. It's extremely important to remember not to touch anything and to avoid standing or leaning on the wreckage, which is often frequented by large, lethal stonefish.

A – Natural construction of alcyonarians in a thousand colors: the uncommonly large dimensions of this one are due to the strong current in this area.

B – The lionfish (Pterois volitans), a skilled predator, is a nocturnal species. During the day, it takes refuge within the stony coral formations.

C – The explosion of colors in the waters of Gobal Seghira attracts numerous visitors, drawn by the brightly colored fish.

B

C

coral formations that provide refuge for large morays (*Gymnothorax javanicus*) and spotted groupers (*Plectropomus pessuliferus*), often intent on being cleaned by small *Stenopus hispidus* shrimp.

Of particular interest are several small caves in the coral wall at a depth of 26 meters. They are a favorite hideaway for schools of glassfish (*Parapriacanthus guentheri*), Lionfish (*Pterois volitans*) and tasseled scorpionfish (*Scorpaenopsis oxycephala*).

D

D – The twobar anemonefish (Amphiprion bicinctus) is associated with various anemones, including Entacmea quadricolor and Heteractis magnifica.

E – A school of blackspotted grunt swims peacefully around the coral pinnacles. Colors and forms merge in this underwater paradise.

F – A lionfish (Pterois volitans) takes refuge under an umbrella Acropora. The underwater world offers sights in a myriad of hues, inhabited by fish with the strangest forms and colors.

Sha'ab Umm Usk

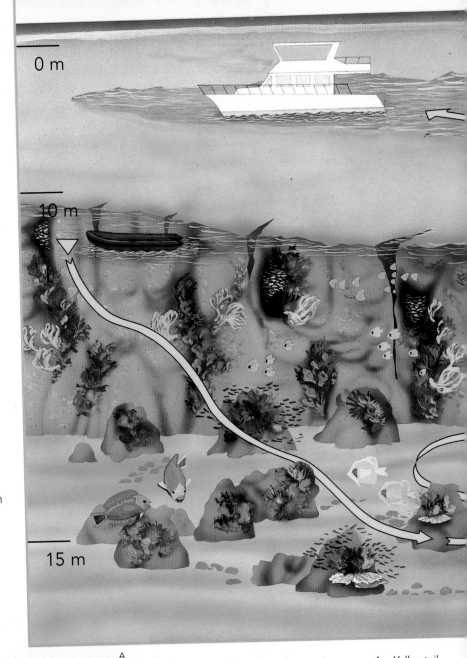

0 m

10 m

15 m

Sha'ab Umm Usk Reef, known in Arabic as "Onghosh," located north of Hurghada between the islands of Big Gobal and Shadwan, consists of a vast, crescent-shaped coral reef over a mile wide. The pass that allows boats to enter the lagoon is located on the western side, where a large coral tower is clearly visible near the entry.

The distinctive horseshoe form of the reef guarantees excellent nighttime anchoring for boats offering cruises in the Straits of Gobal, as the Sha'ab Umm Usk Reef is completely sheltered from the winds that blow primarily from the north. Thus, boats will moor in the lagoon on the southwest side, where the maximum depth is 10 meters. What's special about this reef is the large, permanent pod of bottlenose dolphins (*Tursiops truncatus*) within the lagoon, who make friendly swimming companions on days when the sea is calm. The most interesting place to dive at Sha'ab Umm Usk is the outer side of the west wall. Usually divers use a rubber raft, which takes them about halfway up the reef. From here, jump into the water and follow the wall from north to south, letting the current carry you to the south side of the reef. The seabed, which is between 12 and 16 meters deep, has an extremely varied coral environment with a succession of

A

A – Yellowtail surgeonfish (*Zebrasoma xanthurum*) are a species with an unmistakable bright blue color and brilliant yellow tail. Large schools of them can be observed at shallow depths.

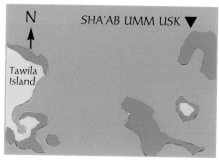

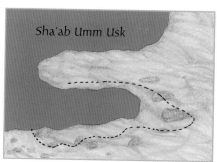

A

A – Bottlenose dolphins live in pods of dozens of individuals. When the dolphins are hunting, every individual in the pod follows precise rules.

B – Sponges, alcyonarians and corals in various forms and colors make the waters of the Red Sea the most spectacular on the planet.

C – Multihued gorgonians make extremely attractive subjects for underwater photos.

B

C brightly colored walls with numerous recesses, providing an ideal refuge for many species of fish. In addition to the extremely interesting coral formations and the wealth of coral fish that enliven the reef, don't forget to look out toward the open sea during your dive. It's not uncommon to see the silvery glint of large pelagic fish like tunas and trevallies in their constant search for food. Just before reaching the end of the reef, you'll see a large cave, which hides schools of small, golden Vanikoro glassfish and cardinal fish. Not far from the cave, at a depth of 15 meters, there are several coral towers. The largest, slightly more isolated and to the south, has walls bursting with branches of alcyonarians, gorgonians, and extremely delicate corals that provide a fine shelter for pennantfish (*Heniochus intermedius*), bluestriped snappers (*Lutjanus kasmira*)

D – Alcyonarians from the Dendronephthya species have an arboreal structure with a translucent, transparent body and colors that range from dark red to pink, white, yellow and violet.

E – Pterois volitans belongs to the Scorpaenidae family, which owe their name to the poisonous spines on the dorsal and ventral fins.

F – The emperor angelfish (Pomacanthus imperator) prefers coral environments full of crevices and little caves. When young, it has a completely different color, with azure-blue tones and white circular stripes.

D

and small *Chromis*, as well as countless varieties of reef fish. Continuing on your dive, you'll come within the shelter of the main reef. After circling it, always keeping to the left side, you'll come to the boat mooring area. Another very

interesting part of the reef is on the northern side. Here, on days when the current is not too strong, you can explore a gently sloping wall with a myriad of stony coral formations.

The best time to dive at Sha'ab Umm Usk is the early afternoon, when the reef is perfectly illuminated by the sun.

The waters of Sha'ab Umm Usk are always more exciting when the sun sets and dark brings on a bustle of activity around the reef. If you dive inside the lagoon, near the pass, you'll be able to glimpse a myriad of creatures within the maze of corals: magnificent Spanish dancers, shrimp, mollusks, crinoids and unique basket stars (*Astroba nuda*), which make excellent subjects for photographs.

F

WRECKS: CARNATIC
GIANNIS D.
TILES

SIYUL SEGHIRA

Shadwan Island

N

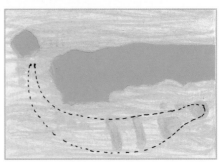

Siyul Seghira

![diagram with depth markers]
0 m

6 m

25 m

A – An octopus (Octopus macropus) *wanders in search of a place to hide.*

B – Dense schools of Vanikoro's sweepers (Parapriacanthus ransonneti) *hover in the shelter of large tropical gorgonians.*

A

B

SIYUL SEGHIRA IS A FLAT ISLAND on the west side of the Gobal channel, west of the larger island of Siyul Kebira.

Although the word "seghira" means "small" in Arabic, the waters around this island hide one of the largest coral reefs in the Straits of Gobal, over four kilometers long and hundreds of meters wide.

South of the island is a large lagoon with a maximum depth of no more than 6 meters, thus creating a zone sheltered from the sea and an excellent mooring place for boats offering cruises in the straits.

The northern side is the most interesting. It is often swept by powerful currents, which encourages the development of a rich biological life.

The best point to start the dive is the outer side of the reef, which is usually reached in a raft, with the cruise boats remaining anchored in the southern lagoon. Dive in just before the lighthouse and follow the reef wall on the right side as it descends gently to a depth of 20-25 meters. Here, you can admire magnificent coral formations comprised of various coral species, primarily Acropora. On the eastern tip of the reef, a few dozen meters away, you can see a coral tower rising up from a depth of 20-25 meters. Its crevices hold a dense school of glassfish (*Parapriacanthus guentheri*), blotcheye soldierfish (*Myripristis murdjan*), and white groupers (*Epinephelus tauvina*).

In the spring, the waters of Siyul

A – This squirrelfish peeps out of its home, dotted with colorful alcyonarians. All around, small anthias rock gently with the current.

B – Commonly known as blackspotted sweetlips, during the day this species of fish lives primarily beneath the rocks. The mating ritual and deposit of eggs takes place in enormous schools that in the end leave a thick, milky layer on the water, due to the enormous quantity of eggs and sperm deposited.

C

D

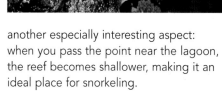

Saghira offer a unique natural spectacle: hundreds of blackspotted grunt (*Plectorhynchus gaterinus*) gather among the corals of this reef, which make a safe, excellent area for reproduction. At the base of the reef, the floor is scattered with small coral formations that continue uninterrupted on the white sand. It's common to see the dark profiles of large morays (*Gymnothorax javanicus*) curiously peeping out of their dens. Continuing your exploration of the sandy areas that open up among the corals, you can spot splendidly camouflaged bluspotted lagoon rays (*Taeniura lymna*) and crocodilefish (*Cociella crocodila*), and more rarely leopard sharks lazily resting on the sea

floor. Not far from the southern tip are two gigantic coral blocks comprised of a countless variety of corals.

The upper zone of the reef is well illuminated by the sun, which sets off its vivacious life and colors. In addition to schools of *Chromis* and anthias, there is a spectacular variety of wrasses, groupers and butterflyfish. This is an ideal place for any photographer who wants magnificent photos of coral fish.

In these crystalline waters you may also see large pelagic fish who have left the deep sea to come to the reef at Siyul in search of prey. The dive ends at the south side of the reef, where the raft waits to help you up to the surface.

The great reef at Siyul also offers

another especially interesting aspect: when you pass the point near the lagoon, the reef becomes shallower, making it an ideal place for snorkeling.

Here, in a maze of corals rising almost to the surface, you can admire the amazing coral life, where thousands of small, vividly colored fish swim close to the surface in an incessant, frenetic activity.

E

C – This blackspotted grouper is very common in the coral reefs and rocky seabeds. It's easy to recognize by the black spot near the top of the head.

D – The goggle-eye (Priacanthus hamrur) lives on the slopes of the reef or in deep lagoons. Its large eyes and bright red color make it easy to recognize.

E – The leopard shark lives primarily on sandy seabeds and is characterized by a long caudal fin. These timid sharks are quite common on the sandy floors of Syul.

Wreck
of
Carnatic

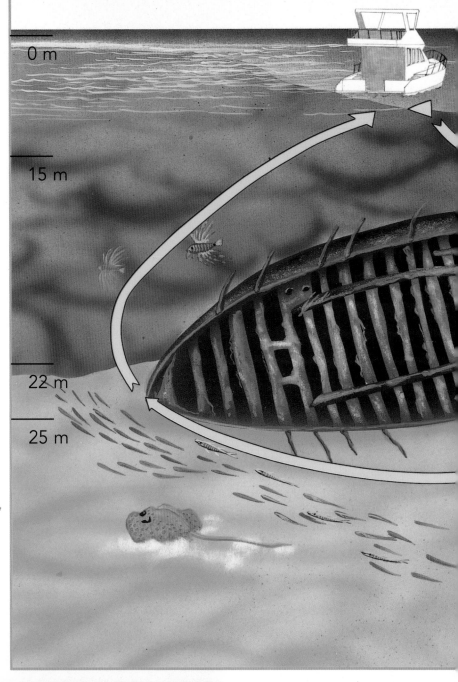

0 m

15 m

22 m

25 m

THE SHA'AB ABU NUHAS REEF lies in the central area of the Straits of Gobal. For many years, especially the decades following the opening of the Suez Canal, it was a real menace to all ships transiting the Gobal channel.

One of the first ships to sink in these waters was the *Carnatic*, whose wreckage is still visible in the waters on the northern side of the Sha'ab Abu Nuhas reef.

The *Carnatic*, launched in 1862, was a fast English vessel 90 meters long, with a tonnage of 1776 tons. What was special about this ship was that it belonged to the first generation of motorized steamships that still had sail fittings, and for this reason was classified as a mixed propulsion steamship. The *Carnatic* was equipped with two large masts and a powerful steam engine, which made the ship quite fast.

The vessel set out from Suez on September 12, 1869, headed for the port of Bombay in India. During this voyage, the ship carried 230 passengers and a cargo of mail for

A

B

A – View from the stern section, now corroded by the sea, but full of sessile fauna that totally covers the metallic structures. In its impact with the reef, the *Carnatic* broke into three pieces.

B – A large alcyonarian has formed at the entrance to the bow section. Colorful micro-organisms have encrusted the ship's bulkhead frames. Salt has corroded the wood, revealing the metal structures.

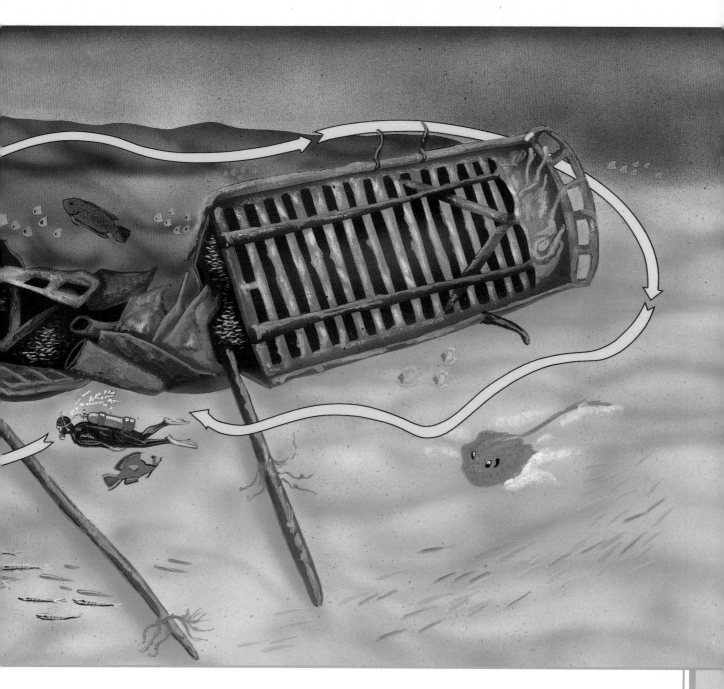

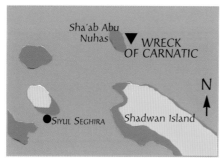

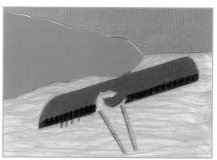

A

B

C

English soldiers in India, as well as numerous bottles of wine and "London Soda Water."

Unfortunately, on the night of September 13, 1869, when it reached the southern end of the Gulf of Suez, the *Carnatic* came dangerously close to the western reefs of the Straits of Gobal, ending its voyage on the sharp corals of Abu Nuhas.

After hitting the reef, the ship remained stranded on top of it, and all efforts to pull it back into the water and restore it to sailing condition failed.

The captain, aware that the ship had not suffered serious damage from the collision, did not immediately give an order to abandon ship, and allowed all passengers to spend the night on board, in hopes of receiving help

A – The stern area of the Carnatic rests on its left side 27 meters deep. From this position, we can see the characteristic rectangular portholes of the ballroom, the enormous rudder, and the massive three-bladed propeller.

B – A diver crosses the upper deck of the Carnatic, colonized by splendid alcyonarians.

C – A century after it sank, the bow is still narrow and pointed, with a soaring line.

D – The interior of one of the holds acts as a permanent home for compact clouds of glassfish, occasionally illuminated by rays of light that filter in from the wreck's portholes.

from the ship *Sumatra*, which, like the *Carnatic*, was from the Peninsular & Oriental Steam Navigation Co.

During the night, the wind began to rise, quickly whipping up enormous waves that violently battered the sides of the *Carnatic*. The hull could not withstand the fury of the sea for long, and the vessel broke in two. The stern area sank immediately, carrying over 20 passengers, while the bow remained wedged on the reef for several months, until a strong gale caused it to slip permanently into the sea at the base of the coral reef.

To dive on the *Carnatic*, the boats should be positioned right

E – An emperor angelfish (Pomacanthus imperator) circles among the structures of the ship near the upper deck. The famous holds lie below. It is said that one of them still contains eight million gold pounds.

F – A sea anemone, in the company of its clownfish, adds life and color to the tragedy of a shipwreck. Through the impetus of reef fish the ship has begun to live again.

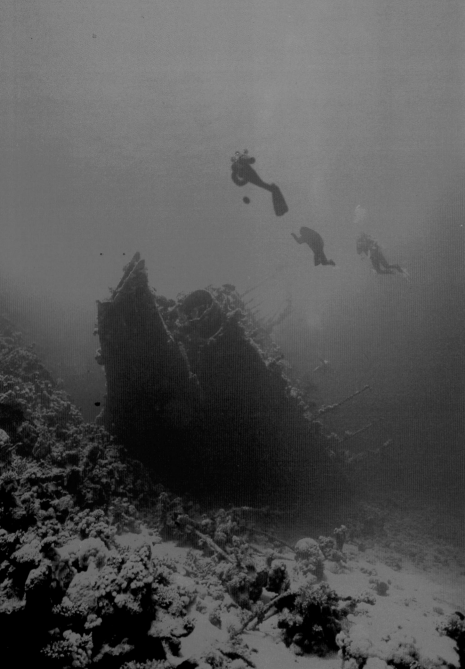

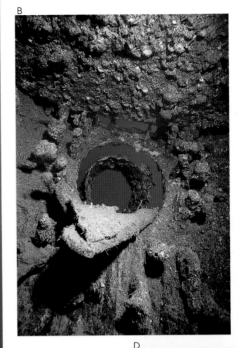

B

A – The bow section is lying on the slope of the reef of Abu Nuhas. In the upper portion, we can see the hole where the bowsprit was attached.

B – A detail of the bowsprit attaching ring taken from the interior of the ship.

D

above the wreck, which is resting on its left side 25 meters down. More than a century after it foundered, the hull is quite corroded by the sea, but due to the rich sessile fauna that totally covers its structures, it is colorful and biologically interesting. After a general exploration around the ship, go down into the stern area, which is one of the most interesting parts of the ship. Here you'll see the massive propeller with three blades. Going on, after crossing the central portion of the ship, which is especially damaged, you'll come to the hold, where there are sturdy metal structures that once

C

C – Bottles of red wine carried in the holds of the Carnatic during its last voyage to the Indies.

Many of these bottles remained unopened for a great number of years.

D – This photo shows the bowsprit ring and support in detail.

E – A blue-lined large eye bream (Monotaxis grandoculis) hovers among the remains of the ship.

F – The classic oval-shaped bottles of Soda Water, with the glass stamped with the names Bombay and Calcutta, the ports of destination.

supported the wooden deck, now totally corroded. In addition, the large cracks among the wreckage, illuminated by the sunlight, create surprising patterns of light. Resting on the sea floor are the two masts, splendidly enveloped with micro-organisms.

Until a few years ago, the cases of wine and the oval cases of Soda Water were still visible in the hold,

the glass stamped with the names Bombay and Calcutta as the ports of destination. Unfortunately, the insensitive habit many divers have of taking souvenirs from wrecks has robbed the *Carnatic* of one of the most fascinating aspects of its history.

G – Some bottles of red wine headed for the English contingent stationed in the colonies of India.

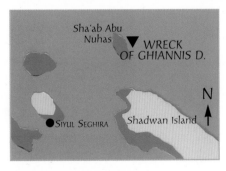

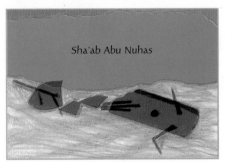

Sha'ab Abu Nuhas ▼ WRECK OF GHIANNIS D.

SIYUL SEGHIRA

Shadwan Island

N

Sha'ab Abu Nuhas

Wreck of Ghiannis D.

A GAIN IN THE WATERS OF ABU NUHAS, not far from the wreck of the *Carnatic*, are the remains of the *Ghiannis D.* A dive on this enormous mercantile ship is extremely interesting, as it is the best preserved ship of the five wrecks near Abu Nuhas. The best time to appreciate the full beauty of the *Ghiannis* is mid-morning, when the clear water and slant of the sunlight illuminate the wreck marvelously.

The *Ghiannis* was a large mercantile ship 100 meters long, with a tonnage of 3000 tons, built in Japan in 1969. It set out for its last voyage from the port of Rijeka, Croatia, in April 1983, bound for the port of Hodeida in Yemen. Due to a probable error in setting its route or for reasons yet unknown, on April 19, 1983 it met the fate of many other ships, colliding with the perilous reef of Abu Nuhas.

Despite the strong impact against the coral reef, the ship did not sink immediately, but remained stranded with its bow on top of the reef, allowing the entire crew to escape in safety.

The hull, battered by the waves that forced it against the sharp corals, did not resist for long. After a few weeks,

0 m

5 m

10 m

22 m

27 m

A – Over the years, a large, delicate pink alcyonarian has encrusted one of the wreck's pulleys.

B – Divers can reach the hold of the Ghiannis D. from the hatches, a detail of which is shown here.

A

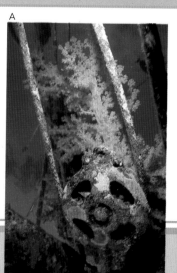

B

A

A – This is a detail of an iron ladder located along one of the ship's bulwarks. Small alcyonarian formations are slowly developing on the iron structures.

B – One of the cargo derricks lying on the sandy floor.

C – The smokestack rises toward the surface. The "D" on the sides stands for the Greek shipping company Danae.

the ship gave way and the *Ghiannis* broke in two and disappeared completely, the two pieces resting on a sandy floor 27 meters deep. Both fell on their left side.

Your exploration of the wreck can begin from the stern, an especially fascinating area, as the ship's structure is still perfectly intact. One of the most interesting aspects is the propeller with its contorted blades, probably due to the collision with the reef.

The poop deck, the bridge and the long guardrail that completely surrounds the stern are quite interesting and make excellent photography subjects. One of the elements that distinguishes the *Ghiannis* is the imposing smokestack stamped with the letter "D," for the Greek shipping company Danae. Across from the smokestack, the mainmast is clearly visible, rising vertically toward the surface, with two large cargo derricks completely enveloped with splendid alcyonarians and clouds of red anthias.

E

D – Thick clusters of alcyonarians cover the base of the Ghiannis D.'s long mast.

E – A general view of the aft area of the Ghiannis D., resting on the sea floor 27 meters deep.

F – Here is a detail of the enormous four-bladed propeller half submerged below the coral surface. In the photo, we can see how the powerful blades contorted as they struck the reef. At the time of the shipwreck, the propeller was moving as the crew desperately tried to steer the ship away from the reef.

G – This long rope hanging from the ship is encrusted with small coral formations.

Countless varieties of coral fish swim around these structures, which are covered with various species of soft corals. You'll see rusty parrotfish (*Scarus ferrugineus*), surgeonfish (*Acanthurus sohal*), sergeant majors (*Abudefduf vaigiensis*), and elegant lionfish (*Pterois volitans*), especially common on the deck below the smokestack. In this area of the hull, you can see several large hatches

F

G

A – Detail of one of the cargo derricks of the Ghiannis D.: magnificent formations of alcyonarians in a thousand colors almost completely envelop the surface.

C – The bow of the Ghiannis D. *is* resting on the port side against the coral reef. Note the long cargo derrick, positioned perfectly on the seabed.

D – The large window in the command tower soars imperiously across from the main deck. Small stony coral formations are taking over the long guardrail.

E – A series of bollards, with a detail shown here, were located along the side of the ship.

D

leading into the interior of the ship.

While exploring this area, carry a powerful flashlight and be extremely careful of the wreckage of the hull, which rust has made quite sharp. The central part of the ship, with the cargo holds, was completely destroyed when the *Ghiannis* broke in two, and now much wreckage is scattered on the sandy floor around the wreck.

If you swim a short distance east, you'll come to the bow section, also perfectly intact and lying on its left side 18 meters deep. Its wreckage offers shelter to schools of glassfish (*Parapriacanthus guentheri*), redmouth groupers (*Aethaloperca rogaa*) and large lunertail groupers (*Variola louti*).

The deck of the bow has two large windlasses. Another unique feature is the two large chains hanging out of the hawsehole. By following the long mast perpendicular to the surface, you'll come to the raft.

E

B – Although the coral is slowly taking over its metallic structures, the ship is in excellent condition. At least two dives are necessary to be able to fully appreciate the wreck's full fascination.

Tile Wreck

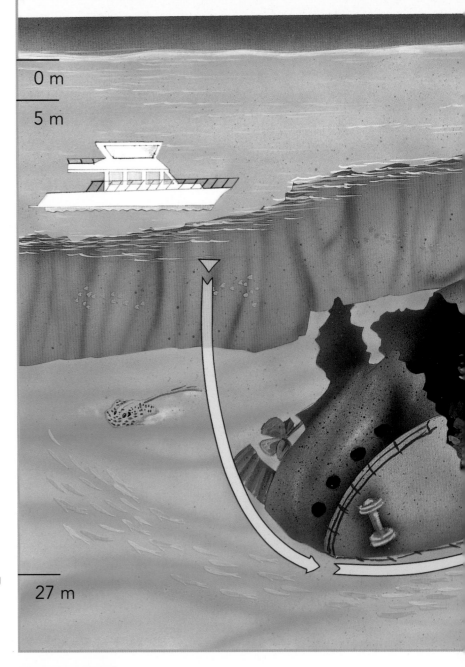

0 m

5 m

27 m

LITTLE IS KNOWN of this enormous mercantile ship mistakenly known as the *Chrisoula K.*, whose bow section now lies on the reef of Abu Nuhas. The bow of this wreck is perfectly intact.

This enormous mercantile ship over 100 meters long, which traversed the waters of the Straits of Gobal in the early 1980s to transport a load of tiles from Italy to ports in Saudi Arabia, followed the fate of other ships, and for reasons still unknown ended its last voyage on the reef of Abu Nuhas.

Probably the causes of the accident were not poor weather conditions that pushed the ship off course, but rather human error. In fact, confirmation of this hypothesis is the great speed with which the ship crashed into the reef of Abu Nuhas, as if the crew responsible for navigation were absolutely sure of their course, and thus certain they were crossing a safe stretch of sea. The violence of the impact was so great that it sank the ship immediately. Fortunately, despite the tremendous impact against the reef, the

entire crew managed to escape safely.

As it sank, the quarter-deck twisted significantly, falling with its right side on the seabed 27 meters deep, while the rest of the ship now lies along the slope of the reef.

Your dive begins right above the wreck, where, as soon as you jump into the water, you'll see the great dark outline of the hull lying on the coral sand perpendicular to the reef. You should

A – The ship is resting on its right side. The quarter-deck, the cargo derricks and the propeller are clearly visible.

B – The contorted wreckage in the stern area testify to the ship's dramatic foundering.

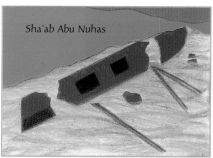

A

B

C

A – One of the cargo derricks lies on the sandy floor 30 meters deep. All around, we can see parts of the ship that scattered on the floor as it sank.

B – The ship's cargo consisted of tiles made in Italy. Within the hold are cases containing the cargo, sometimes illuminated by shafts of light filtering through the openings.

begin your exploration from the deepest area, where you will find the stern with the four-bladed propeller and rudder still visible. Together, they make an interesting shot for a photograph. Continuing along the starboard side and rising to shallower depths, one of the long cargo derricks will appear before you, lying on the floor. A little further on, at a depth of 19 meters, you'll find the smokestack. Garden eels, a sort of snake, appear from the sandy floor, standing up in a vertical position. Continuing your dive along the deck, you'll reach the hold openings, where you can see the cargo of tiles "Made in Italy," heaped chaotically within the hull due to the impact with the reef. Being careful not to stir up the thin layer of mud

C – The aft mast of the wreck, in excellent condition, is lying on its right side. As we go on, we see how the violent crash against the reef of Abu Nuhas severely twisted the wreckage.

D – Here is a general view of the ship's aft mast, lying on the right side. We can see the enormous rudder and large propeller rising out of the sea bed, with signs of the violent collision.

E – The enormous smokestack, which snapped off the ship due to the strong impact against the reef, is lying on the sandy floor. Groups of colorful coral fish live inside it.

F – The bow of the ship, from which the anchor chain is hanging, is encrusted onto the top of the reef just a few meters deep.

in the hold, go to the engine room, dominated by the great, now silent 12 cylinder engine. Even now, covered with rust, it still exudes a clear aura of mechanical power. You can also see various pieces of work equipment scattered here and there.

A flashlight is absolutely necessary to explore the interior of the ship, as the dim light that penetrates the portholes and cargo hatches is not sufficient to illuminate the interior.

The interior of the hold is especially spectacular due to the dense schools of glassfish swiftly darting through the shadows, while the outside wreckage has already been colonized by various sessile creatures, which, along with coral fish, wreathe the entire wreck with color. Going on, you'll come to the bow section, where you can see schools of *Platax* hovering in the water.

Moving toward the wall of the reef, you'll see the bow bulwarks resting on the sea floor and a variety of contorted wreckage. In the shelter of the bow, resting on the floor, you will find the hawsehole with the anchor chain hanging from it. On the surface of the reef, note the deep dent caused by the ship's strong impact, proof of the violence with which the vessel crashed into the reef of Abu Nuhas. You should dive in the afternoon, when the entire deck of the ship is illuminated.

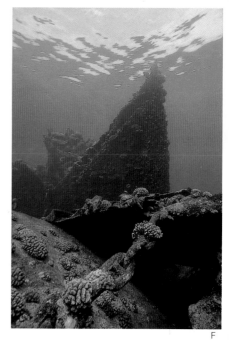

F

N

▼ SHA'AB EL ERG

● ISLAND OF
   UMM GAMAR

SHABRUR ●
UMM GAMAR

Hurghada ↘

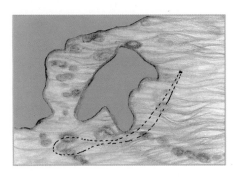

A – Siderea grisea is a moray that may reach 50 centimeters long.

B – The Red Sea pennantfish (Heniochus intermedius) is a territorial creature.

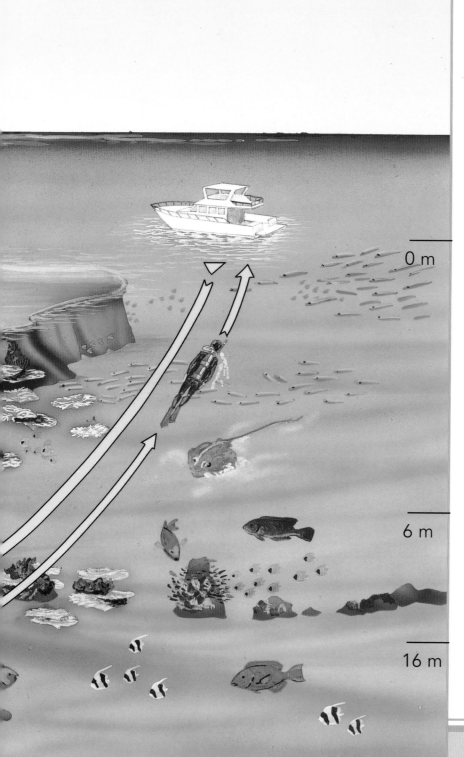

Gotha Sha'ab el Erg

LOCATED NORTHWEST OF THE ISLAND of Shadwan, Sha'ab el Erg is a large reef that is easily recognizable by its horseshoe shape. Within it, well protected from the north winds, is a vast lagoon that provides a safe mooring place for boats. One of the features of Sha'ab el Erg is the presence of a sedentary pod of bottlenose dolphins (*Tursiops truncatus*) in the lagoon. Bottlenoses are curious creatures, and the pod will often swim around the moored boats to watch the humans on them.

Something else you should watch for is the giant mantas (*Manta birostris*) you can see on the north side of the reef from January to March.

Not far from the southwest tip of Sha'ab el Erg, you can see the top of a small reef known as Gotha Sha'ab el Erg, an extremely interesting diving area. Here, boats can moor at the buoys anchored on the southern side.

A dive at Gotha Sha'ab el Erg will remain within depths of 6 to 16 meters, following the southern perimeter until you reach the channel that separates it

0 m

6 m

16 m

A

B

A – The yellowsaddle goatfish (Parupeneus cyclostomus) is easily recognizable by its gaudy color and long barbels with their powerful chemical sensors, which it uses to find food hidden on the sea floor.

B – One of the most beautiful and unforgettable encounters you can experience during a dive is with dolphins, who will allow divers to approach them and admire their extraordinary maneuvers and playful movements.

C – Scalefine anthias (Pseudanthias squamipinnis), which are only a few centimeters long, densely populate every stretch of the coral reef. With their bright red-orange color, they create magical scenes.

from the main reef of Sha'ab el Erg. The route is technically easy, as it follows the base of the reef along a maze of coral formations. Entering the water directly from the boat moored to the buoys, follow the edge of the reef west until you reach a sort of coral blade that extends gently out to the open sea.

This is a good place to admire vast, massive, magnificently colored coral formations, from delicate yellow fire corals (Millepora dichotoma) to brilliant violet raspberry corals (Pocillopora verrucosa). The sea floor is especially bright, both due to the shallow depth and the crystalline water, which sets off

dense schools of fish moving symmetrically along the reef. In the more sheltered cracks among the corals, it's not uncommon to see schools of glassfish with redmouth groupers (Aethaloperca rogaa) strategically hidden among them waiting for some unwary prey. Continuing your dive, move slightly away from the southern tip of Gotha and come to several coral pinnacles rising up from the sandy floor, where you can take some fine photos.

Around the towers, you can see the frenetic activity of small reef fish like anthias. Observe them closely to discover the dynamic secrets of coral life.

A wide variety of coral fish and other splendid coral formations enrich the scene in these waters. Gazing out to the open sea, you can often admire schools

of trevallies and small fusiliers as well.

The sandy areas are also interesting, creating a sort of clearing among the corals where you can find bluespotted lagoon rays intently rummaging in the sand, as well as crocodilefish (cociella crocodilla), remnants of careless prehistory. Triggerfish (Balistoides viridescens) also populate these waters, and with a bit of luck you may see some rare gray morays (Siderea grisea) sheltered among the large Acropora corals. Once in a while you may encounter a nurse shark lying lazily on the sandy floor. These are all excellent opportunities for macrophotography, where you can use your lens to enlarge and set off the small creatures that enliven the waters of Gotha Sha'ab el Erg.

C

D – The most common family of stony corals on the floors of the Red Sea is certainly the Acropora, which include about fifteen different species. Acropora reproduction takes place at precise times of the year, when the coral releases enormous quantities of gametes that color the sea pink.

E – The crocodile fish (cociella crocodila) owes its name to the shape of its head and its large mouth. It frequents sandy

D

E

areas at the base of the reef, where it lies on the sea floor in wait for some unwary prey.

F – Scalefine anthias (Pseudanthias squamipinnis) live in harems of one male and about ten females. If the male dies, sexual inversion takes place and one of the females will change sex and color to take his place.

El Gouna

TWENTY-TWO KILOMETERS NORTH of Hurghada is the magnificent, brand new El Gouna vacation center, a unique group of artificial lagoons reflecting sober, elegant buildings that overall create an unusual Venice along the shores of the Red Sea. The El Gouna residential complex has been skillfully inserted into a dream landscape: to the west are the desert slopes of the Crystalline Mountains, while to the east is a coastline formed of an archipelago of little islands, lagoons and channels, where the sea becomes turquoise blue. Until a few years ago, this area had absolutely no tourist facilities and its coasts were nothing but a series of lonely inlets. On days when the strong north wind made fishing difficult, fishermen used the coast as a well-protected shelter.

Today the landscape has changed completely, and in just a few years this evocative district has sprung up; an independent little town where luxurious villas, apartments, hotels and restaurants blend together in a harmonious architectural style that respects the surrounding environment. Within this futuristic framework are hotels like the Movenpick, the Sonesta Paradisio, the Sheraton Miramar, and many others, all connected by a network of navigable canals and bridges. El Gouna contains a whole series of logistical services, including a small airport, a modern, well-equipped hospital and a school, making this town a true model of practicality serving tourists and local residents.

This unique place was designed and built after an in-depth evaluation of the environmental impact the residential structures would have on the surrounding land. During construction, enormous importance was placed on the existing features of the territory and the landscape. The agricultural area in the shelter of the mountains, for example, was conserved and improved, transforming it into a model cooperative specializing in agricultural and food products. The agricultural methods of the Nubian cultures in the Nile Valley were left unchanged.

Now El Gouna has one of the most practical, modern tourist centers on the Egyptian coast, with several highly professional diving centers that organize daily trips to the areas north of the Hurghada archipelago. There are numerous diving areas, all of which are extremely interesting: Sha'ab abu Galawa, Umm Gamar, Careless Reef and others.

As El Gouna is not far from the islands of Shadwan and Gobal, you can even go on daily dives in fast boats that will take you to the shipwrecks at Sha'ab Abu Nuhas.

In addition, with the aid of expert local guides, you can organize

A – Entering the monastery, a maze of narrow lanes leads to a spring of fresh, pure water. The monastery has an excellent irrigation system that uses every last drop of water.

B - A panoramic view of the Nubian Village of El Gouna, built on an isthmus of land surrounded by cobalt blue water.

C - The St. Anthony Monastery is located in Gebel Hammamat, in the desert 300 kilometers north of Hurghada. The monastery looks like a mirage, with high walls adorned by cupolas and towers.

D- A friendly striped dolphin swims freely in the transparent waters off the island of Umm Gamar. These magnificent animals often appear unexpectedly during a dive.

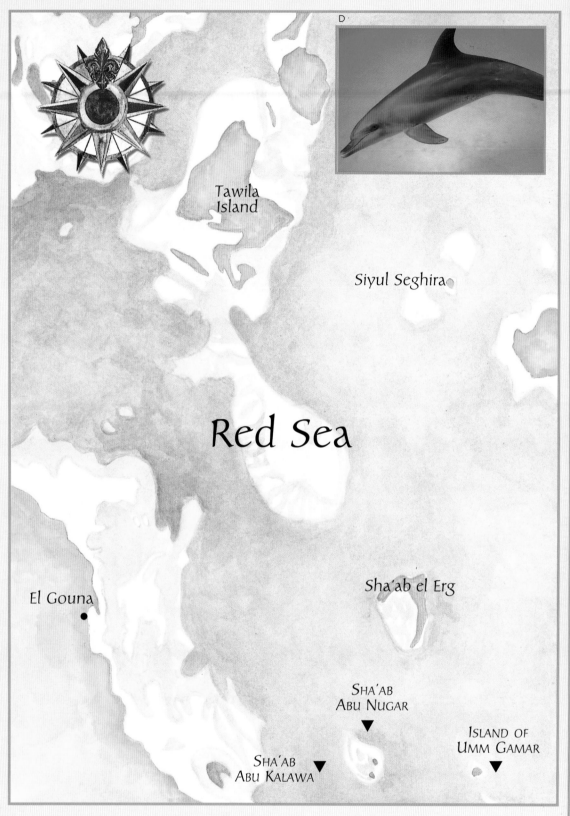

D

Tawila Island

Siyul Seghira

Red Sea

Sha'ab el Erg

El Gouna

SHA'AB ABU NUGAR

ISLAND OF UMM GAMAR

SHA'AB ABU KALAWA

fantastic excursions to the desert, where you can see Bedouin villages and discover interesting aspects of the ancient nomadic culture.

Another interesting trip is a visit to the Coptic monasteries of St. Anthony and St. Paul, located about 250 kilometers to the north in the heart of the desert, accessible by the road to Suez. According to tradition, these monasteries were founded in the early 4th century AD by the hermits Anthony and Paul, who lived in this desert area in total meditative solitude.

From El Gouna, the first monastery you'll see is St. Anthony. With its majestic walls, cupolas and high towers, it almost looks like a mirage. The underground crypts of the two monasteries, just a few dozen kilometers apart, offer ancient frescoes and fascinating areas where daily monastic life goes on.

The sophisticated El Gouna complex offers visitors other activities, such as an excellent golf course and riding school, so travelers can enjoy a complete, relaxing vacation.

Sha'ab Abu Nugar

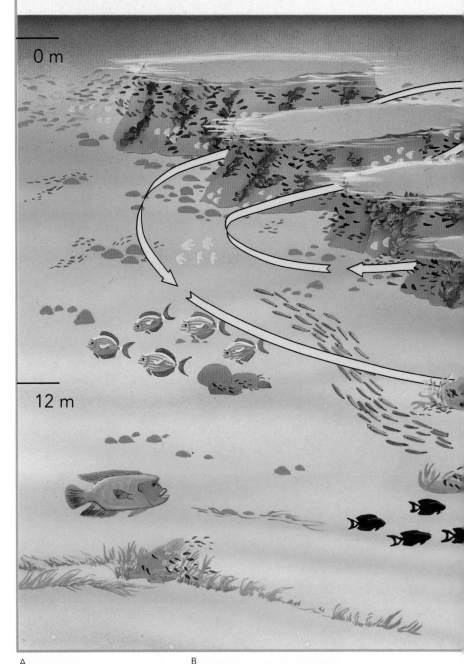

0 m

12 m

THE SHA'AB ABU NUGAR CORAL REEF, which is about a 30 minute sail from El Gouna, has a distinctive elongated form; the east side is dotted with an innumerable succession of coral towers rising from the seabed to almost the water's surface.

The areas between the columns create excellent shelters from wind and sea; indeed, in the local language the name Sha'ab Abu Nugar means "father of pools," due to the tranquil lagoons that have formed among these corals.

The most interesting area to explore is southwest of the main reef, where there are several massive coral towers like those at Gotha Abu Nugar and Sha'ab Iris, which include a group of essentially pristine reefs.

You'll begin your dive at the outer edge of the reef. Once you've reached the base at 12 meters, proceed north to discover numerous spectacular passages among the corals in this splendid underground garden. The luminous water and currents carrying in plankton create ideal conditions for the growth and development of countless organisms that constantly enliven this reef, populated by various species of Steephead parrotfish (*Scarus gibbus*), surgeonfish (*Acanthurus sohal*), small gobies and innumerable wrasses, who will attract the curiosity of any diver. In the first few meters down,

A

B

A – The colorful pennantfish (Heniochus intermedius), a member of the Chaetonidae family, becomes darker at night.

B – Swimming along the wall of a reef is like flying over a fantastic, unreal landscape.

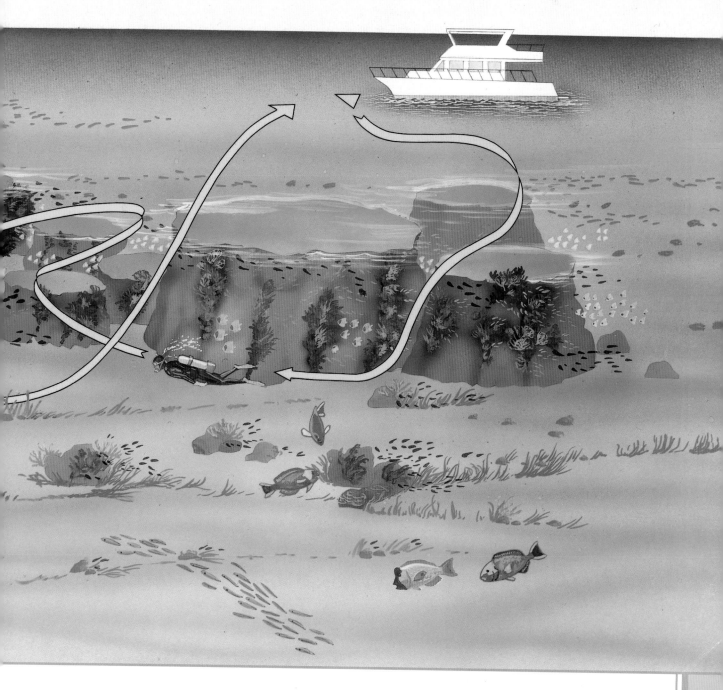

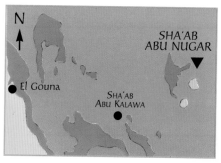

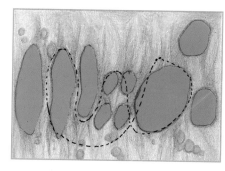

SHA'AB ABU NUGA

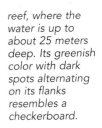

A – The horny skeleton of the gorgonians is extremely flexible, allowing them to bend without breaking in the flow of sea currents.

B – The checkerboard wrasse (Halichoeres hortulanus) frequents sandy seabeds near the reef, where the water is up to about 25 meters deep. Its greenish color with dark spots alternating on its flanks resembles a checkerboard.

C – By day, the grape coral (Plerogyra sinuosa) displays bladders that retract when the animal is disturbed. At night, the coral's polyps emerge, with tentacles that capture nourishing substances in the dark.

the reef area is colonized primarily by Acropora corals with short, stout branches, a structure that makes these corals more resistant to the waves. As you go farther down, you'll see more branching corals, because at these depths the hydrodynamic effect of the waves decreases significantly, creating ideal conditions for the growth of most types of stony corals.

The different coral structures form a sort of large calcareous garden that grows together to slowly raise the reef up toward the surface.

There may be tens of thousands of tiny polyps in a single coral, and one small reef can contain hundreds of corals, held securely together by an immense, complicated calcareous architecture. As you near the reef, notice the details of the corals by observing the little polyps with their delicate crowns of tentacles ceaselessly opening and closing in order to capture the micro-organisms that are so vital for their nourishment.

The single-celled zooxanthellae algae in each polyp are vitally important. Numerous studies by marine biologists have shown how this type of algae is crucial to coral metabolism, as it favors the deposition of calcium carbonate and the consequent formation of the coral's calcareous skeleton. The microscopic zooxanthellae need a significant quantity of light to develop, and for this very reason, clear water is indispensable to the life of the reef. Banks of corals struggle to survive in deep water where there is not enough sunlight for the growth of zooxanthellae.

As you dive among this maze of coral columns, you'll soon see that each one has different characteristics, depending on the type of current running past it.

At Sha'ab Abu Nugar, you could spend hours observing the extraordinary spectacle its tangle of corals offers. But time passing will bring you brusquely back to reality, and you'll need to re-surface.

E – Goniopora colonies can become extremely large. The polyps that form them are long and cylindrical, with 24 small tentacles at their tips.

F – With their diverse forms and sizes, the stony corals of the reef may resemble branching trees or large globular masses.

D – Red Sea pennantfish (Heniochus intermedius) have an extremely elongated fourth ray of the dorsal fin, with bright yellow and black bands.

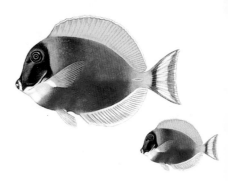

A – The coral grouper (Cephalopholis miniata) with *its* splendid bright red color and blue spots, forms harems of one male and numerous females (from 3 to 10).

Sha'ab Abu Kalawa

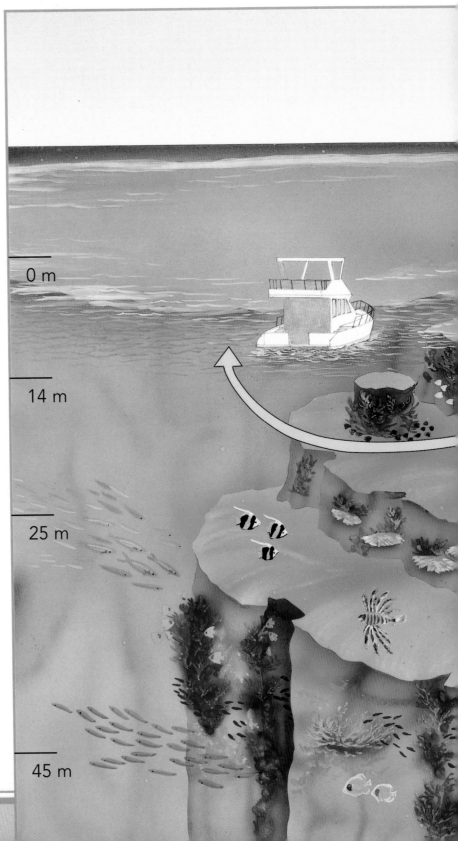

0 m

14 m

25 m

45 m

SHA'AB ABU KALAWA IS A REEF located 30 minutes away from El Gouna. The diving area is located along the south side of the reef. You'll need to do a drift dive on the east side of the reef, then follow the current and emerge in the tranquil waters of the south side, where the diving center boat will be waiting for you.

The reef consists of a wall descending over 50 meters, broken by large terraces. This special conformation creates a lovely, unusual environment, where you can observe various forms of life, from coral fish to large gorgonians to pelagic fish swimming off in the blue depths.

Right from the start, this wall is especially full of coral and interesting crevices that run from the top of the reef and descend vertically for many meters.

As you explore these cracks, you can discover a wide variety of sedentary fish like groupers (*Plectropomus pessuliferus*), lionfish (*Pterois volitans*), and delicate schools of pennantfish (*Heniochus intermedius*).

When you reach a depth of 14 meters, you'll see the first coral plateau below you. Several coral towers rise up

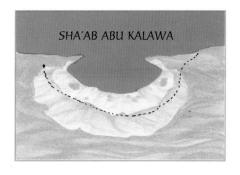

SHA'AB ABU KALAWA

A

B from it, full of alcyonarians, soft corals and gorgonians, while the base of the plateau is completely covered with gigantic, perfectly intact umbrella Acropora formations. The whole area also offers numerous sponges in various shapes, such as *Siphonochalina siphonella*, consisting of a group of long, pale violet tubes.

As you move south, you'll reach the far end of the plateau, where the reef drops another ten meters or so and then immediately forms another plateau at a depth of 25 meters, which stretches out into the deep blue sea like a fantastic natural balcony.

Along the wall, right from the start you can see various cavities and caves, within which are redmouth groupers

(Aethaloperca rogaa), Clearfin lionfish (Pterois radiata) and blackspotted grunt (Plectorhinchus gaterinus). Another fascinating feature is the large sea fans (Subergorgia hicksoni) and long branches of black coral (Cirripathes anguina) which, especially after about 20 meters deep, become dense and especially luxuriant.

From the outside edge of this second terrace, you'll come to the vertical drop, where reef life becomes more intense. It feels like you're on a sort of platform overlooking a moving theater where the primordial spectacle of totally pristine underwater life is played out ceaselessly before your eyes.

Sometimes, when the current is stronger, you may see an even finer sight as dense schools of pelagic fish, heedless of divers, take advantage of the abundant food and move to the edges of the reef.

You don't need to dive deep, as you can see extremely interesting life forms even within the first 28 meters if you move away from the terrace a bit. Every inch of space seems crammed with organisms you should watch carefully. Take the time to observe for a few minutes so you can understand their biological dynamics. You should take this dive early in the afternoon, when sunlight fully illuminates the wall.

Large gorgonians open majestically to the current to capture the precious plankton, whip corals oscillate, reaching out to the light, and an extraordinary abundance of corals prospers along the entire wall. Sometimes you may be lucky enough to see schools of barracudas swimming off in the blue depths, helping to create a magical underwater environment.

F – The delicate movements of the Spanish dancer (Hexabranchus sanguineus) are reminiscent of a flamenco dancer. During reproduction, they deposit their eggs in slender bands of mucus.

A – The clearfin lionfish (Pterois radiata), a member of the Scorpaenidae family, has poisonous spines that it uses for defense.

B – The Siphonochalina siphonella sponge is a reddish porifer with a structure similar to a pipe organ. In this photo, it has grown among the branches of a fire coral (Millepora dichotoma).

C – The giant grouper (Epinephelus tauvina) frequents the sandy areas among the stony corals, where it camouflages itself perfectly.

D – Crinoids (which are echinoderms) are commonly seen during night dives.

E – Pseudanthias taeniatus live in dense schools among the corals, where they will take refuge at the slightest sign of danger.

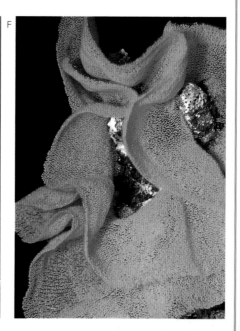

Island of Umm Gamar

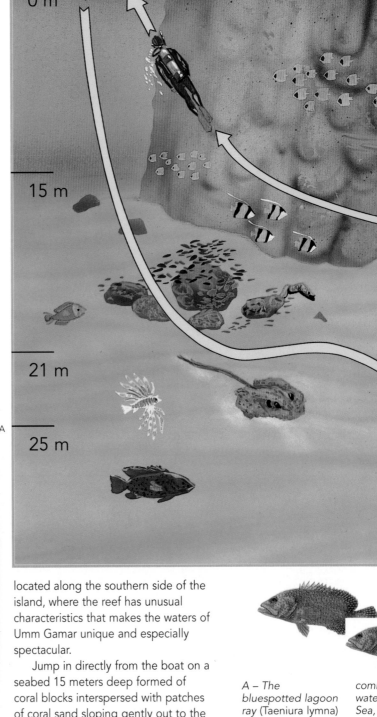

0 m

15 m

21 m

A

25 m

T HE ISLAND OF UMM GAMAR, which in Arabic means "mother of the moon," is the northernmost diving area in the Hurghada archipelago, and is especially easy to reach from El Gouna. This small island, easily identifiable by the small lighthouse, is the emerging tip of a vast reef that extends north to south for hundreds of meters. Boats from diving centers can moor at the buoys located in the shelter of the island's southern side, so that they won't destroy the reef's fragile coral structures with their anchors.

The most interesting diving area is

located along the southern side of the island, where the reef has unusual characteristics that makes the waters of Umm Gamar unique and especially spectacular.

Jump in directly from the boat on a seabed 15 meters deep formed of coral blocks interspersed with patches of coral sand sloping gently out to the open sea. As you explore the coral formations at the base of the wall, you'll see large morays (Gymnothorax

A – The bluespotted lagoon ray (Taeniura lymna) with its splendid gray-yellowish color and blue spots, is quite common in the waters of the Red Sea, especially in sandy areas at the base of the reef or within coastal lagoons.

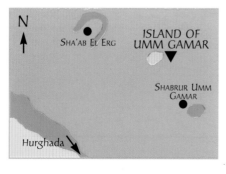

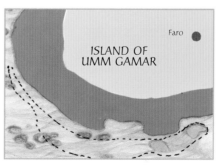

A – The giant grouper (Epinephelus tauvina) grouper is a powerful territorial predator; excessive, indiscriminate fishing of this species could cause imbalances in the reef ecosystem.

B – The redmouth grouper (Aethaloperca rogaa) is common in deep fissures, where it is perfectly camouflaged in the dark caves.

javanicus) peeping curiously out of their dens at the sound of your approach.

Following the long eastern wall northwards, the seabed creates a wide coral terrace with four large coral towers traversed by deep, beautiful recesses.

The first tower, located a few dozen meters from the mooring point, rises majestically up from a depth of about 21 meters. With the aid of a flashlight, you can see the iridescent colors of various species of gorgonians and a multitude of glassfish

(Parapriacanthus guentheri) oscillating in a harmonious, compact mass in the rays of light that filter down from the top of the cave. Proceeding with the wall to the left, you'll come to the second tower, distinguished by a large recess at a depth of 25 meters, within which there are redmouth groupers (Aethaloperca rogaa), glassfish, a large school of lionfish (Pterois volitans) and stonefish (Synanceia verrucosa) skillfully camouflaged on the seabed.

On top of the pinnacle you can see

large gorgonians and alcyonarians with numerous arms reaching out to the blue depths. Schools of small trevallies (Carangoides bajad) often swim around this tower, heedless of divers as they pursue their prey and create havoc among the small coral fish, who rush for shelter in the crevices of the reef.

The third tower, more slender in form, is located just beyond. It has an opening at the base near a sandy plateau, an ideal place to watch the mimetic crocodilefish

C – The yellowsaddle goatfish (Parupeneus cyclostomus) feeds on small fish that it hunts in the coral crevices, using its long barbels as sensors.

D – Gorgonians are fan-shaped colonial forms that develop perpendicular to the current, allowing the small polyps to capture the plankton that forms the basis of their diet.

E – The yellowbar angelfish (Pomacanthus maculosus) has a color that can change as it matures.

F – The island of Umm Gamar is one of the most famous diving areas in the entire Hurghada archipelago.

(Cociella crocodila), spotted eagle rays (Aetobatus narinari), and even a few tasseled scorpionfish (Scorpaenopsis oxycephala).

To reach the fourth and final tower, follow the terrace that gently rises toward the surface to a depth of 12 meters. If you peer into the cavity, you'll see large lionfish (Pterois volitans), giant groupers (Epinephelus tauvina), and the ever-present glassfish.

Return to the boat on the right side of the wall, where, closer to the surface, you can admire the wealth of biological life along the entire Umm Gamar coral reef. The best time for diving is the morning or early afternoon, when the sunlight illuminates the whole wall, its rays filtering down into the caves.

During your exploration, don't enter these small recesses, where you may inadvertently break fragile coral formations, but simply observe from the mouth of the cave.

A
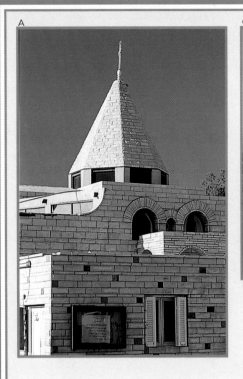

C

Hurghada

B

THE TOWN OF HURGHADA, located on the western coast of the Egyptian Red Sea, 600 kilometers south of Cairo, stands on the site of the ancient port of Myos Hormos, which during the Ptolemaic period was an important trading center for goods coming from the desert.

In the early 1970s, the little town of Hurghada was known to a small

D

elite of travelers willing to face countless inconveniences to reach the virgin coasts of the Red Sea. At that time, Hurghada was the only place to dive in this sea full of pelagic fish. Then, in the late 1970s, following President Sadat's efforts to boost tourism and the economy, Hurghada steadily grew, and by the second half of the 1980s had gradually transformed itself from a small fishing village into an agglomerate of hotels that now offer exceptional accommodations. The long desert coast is now dotted with modern hotels from the world's leading tourism chains, and this is where almost all European tourists who visit the Red Sea stay. The reason for this rapid development is

A – The modern Coptic Christian church is located in the center of the town of Hurghada, where it co-exists with the Islamic faith, quite common in a city that can nevertheless be considered multi-ethnic.

B – At sunset, the minarets of Hurghada's mosque, a symbol of tradition, and the great high voltage pylons, a sign of encroaching progress.
In the background, the magical light of the sun setting behind the mountains.

C – Hurghada is rapidly growing and transforming. All that remains of the old urban fabric is a few characteristic streets and the unchanging clear skies.

D – The characteristic port area is still the heart of the town, and has remained unchanged despite the great influx of tourists. Only the shipbuilding industry has changed, with small boats supplanted by large scuba diving vessels.

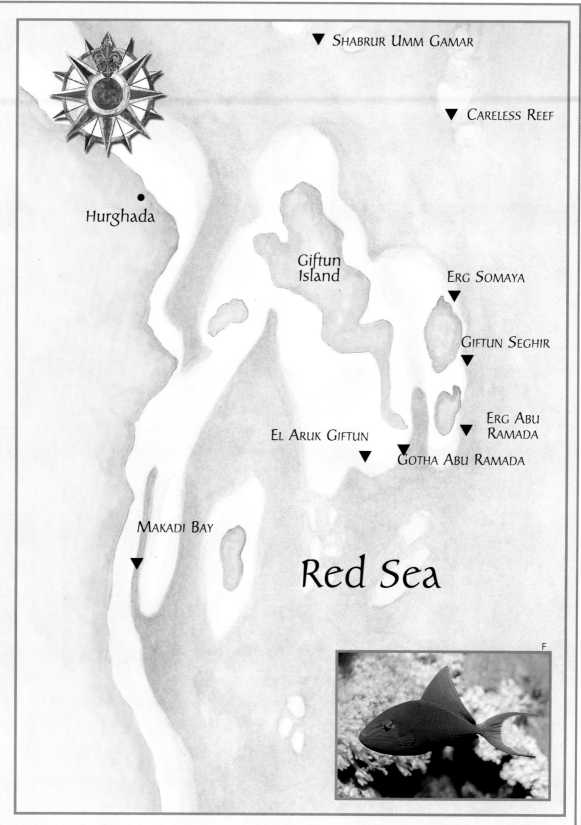

▼ SHABRUR UMM GAMAR

▼ CARELESS REEF

Hurghada

Giftun Island

ERG SOMAYA
▼

GIFTUN SEGHIR
▼

ERG ABU RAMADA
▼

EL ARUK GIFTUN
▼

GOTHA ABU RAMADA

MAKADI BAY
▼

Red Sea

F

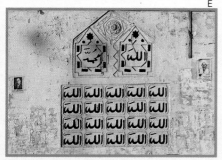

E – The eastern wall of the old mosque in the heart of the town is covered with prayers sculpted in the pink rock, arranged in geometric designs according to Islamic tradition.

F – The redtooth triggerfish (Odonus niger) lives mostly in schools. During the reproductive season, it digs large holes in the sandy floor to lay its eggs.

primarily the coastal conformation, which creates a wide inlet right in front of the town, crowned by an archipelago of numerous islands and reefs.

This feature has made it possible for the numerous diving centers that have sprung up around Hurghada's hotels to organize daily excursions

A – Large Giftun Island has the splendid beach of Mahmya, well equipped to offer a day of total relaxation in the turquoise waters of the Red Sea.

B – In the channel that separates Small Giftun from the large island, the turquoise and cobalt tones of the sea blend into a single palette of color.

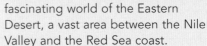

to over 20 diving areas. Accessible in short boat trips, the beauty of these diving areas has made this place worldwide famous.

The waters of Hurghada offer different types of dives, from descents along walls that drop off into the abyss to dives around shallows and solitary reefs.

Most of the archipelago's diving sites are within a half hour's sail. You can dive in the waters of Gotha Abu Ramada, Erg Abu Ramada, Aruk Giftun, and many shallow enough to be considered true aquariums, inhabited by a multitude of brilliantly colored coral fish who have now become accustomed to the presence of humans. In addition, there are the islands of Giftun Kebira, Giftun Seghira and Abu Ramada, where you can discover the splendid coral walls of

C – The blackspotted grunts (Plectorhinchus gaterinus) reaches a length of 40 centimeters, and lives in small schools. It has a robust body and a rounded head. It is silvery in color, with yellow fins, and the entire body is covered with small dark spots.

D – A school of Pterois volitans floats at the mouth of a cave. Don't be deceived by the harmless-looking indolence of these splendid fish. If disturbed, they can mount a swift attack, causing their hapless victim painful injuries.

Giftun drift, North Abu Ramada and Erg Somaya.

Sailing about an hour north, you'll come to the island of Umm Gamar, famous for its coral towers, Shabrur Umm Gamar, and Careless Reef, the undisputed realm of giant morays.

Just a little farther away are numerous shipwrecks in the waters of the Straits of Gobal, an obligatory passage for ships from the Suez Canal. Due to the enormous variety of underwater environments, Hurghada has for years been one of the most famous diving areas of the world.

A trip to Hurghada offers not only the sea and splendid diving, but also unforgettable excursions to the

fascinating world of the Eastern Desert, a vast area between the Nile Valley and the Red Sea coast.

This is an area full of evocative landscapes that hold various archaeological remains of the ancient peoples who passed through and lived in these desert lands. It is a mysterious place, full of traces of the history of ancient Egypt, where Egyptians and Romans created magnificent works that are still perfectly preserved to this day, and semi-precious stones and porphyry

E – A school of bluefin trevallies (Caranx melampygus) swims on the outer side of the reef. Encounters with this species of fish are quite common during dives.

were mined to build imposing Roman temples.

The only way you can discover this fascinating, mysterious land is through the experience and knowledge of local guides who organize jeep excursions to the desert that protects the town of Hurghada, now dizzily poised for a leap into the future.

A and B – The coral grouper (Cephalopholis miniata), *which can reach up to a half a meter in length, has a splendid red color with small blue spots over its entire body. This member of the Serranidae family prefers coral reefs with tall stony coral formations it can use for shelter.*

Shabrur Umm Gamar

THIS DIVING AREA, located less than three kilometers south of the island of Umm Gamar, consists of an extensive shallows running northwest and southeast.

Your dive begins right from the boat, moored to the buoys anchored on the south side of the reef.

Once in the water, you'll come to a white sand floor 16 meters deep, scattered with various stony and other coral formations. Particularly lovely is a large stony coral pinnacle that rises from the floor up to six meters from the surface, its walls completely covered with gorgonians and alcyonarians. At the base is a small cave, inhabited by a magnificent moray (*Gymnothorax javanicus*). With a little luck, you may also see a large grouper (*Epinephelus summana*) resting on the floor or camouflaged among the rocks. Continuing your dive with the reef to your left, you'll come to the southeast side of the shallows, which slopes down to form a terrace

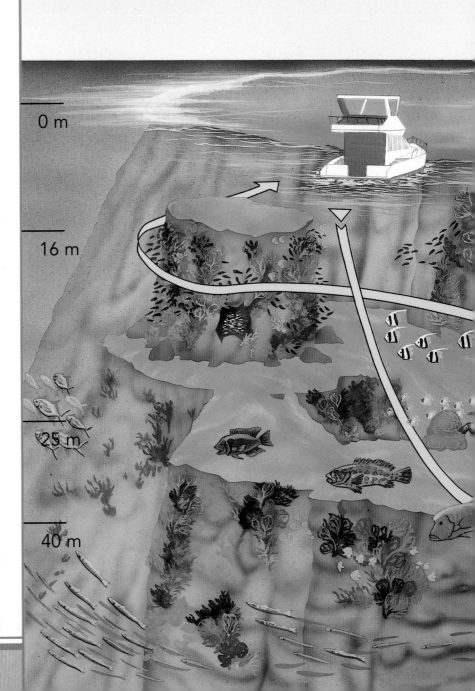

0 m

16 m

25 m

40 m

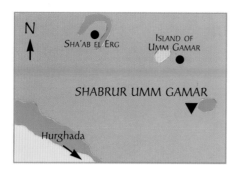

Sha'ab el Erg

Island of
Umm Gamar

SHABRUR UMM GAMAR

Hurghada

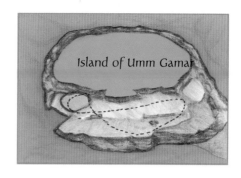

Island of Umm Gamar

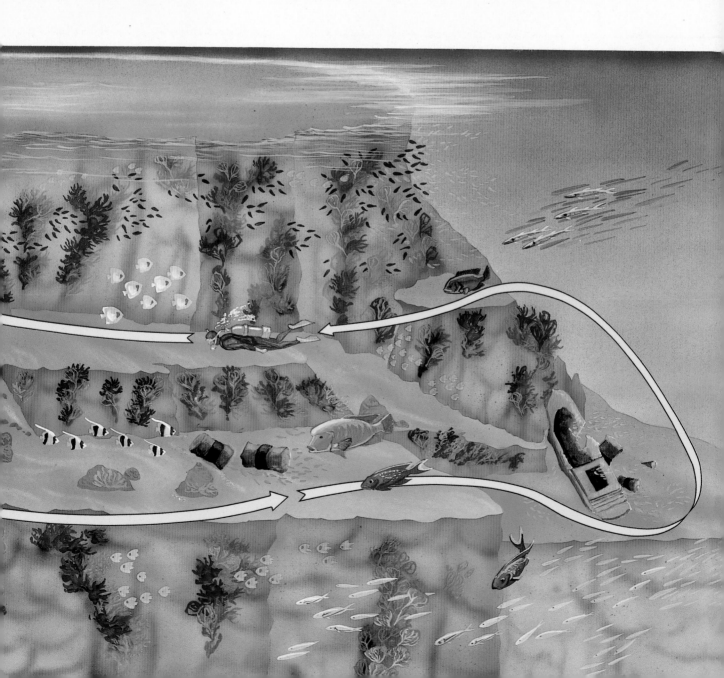

A

A – The camouflage grouper (Epinephelus polyphekadion) prefers lagoons or coastal areas sheltered from the reefs.

B – A large giant moray (Gymnothorax javanicus) remains perfectly motionless as a small cleaner wrasse (Labroides dimiatus) removes parasites from its scales.

C – Exploring the interior of a cave, we can admire extraordinary scenes created by rays of sunlight filtering into the cavities.

D – The luneratil grouper (Variola louti), with its red scales, large falcate tail and fins edged in yellow, is one of the most beautiful and elegant members of the Serranidae family in these waters.

E – Bluefin trevallies (Caranx melampygus) travel great distances in a constant search for food, which they capture by using extremely effective pack strategies.

F – The titan triggerfish (Balistoides viridescens) lives primarily in sandy areas near the coral reef. During the reproductive period, when it is protecting its eggs on the sea floor, it can become extremely aggressive.

B

C

30 meters deep. Here the wall becomes steep and drops vertically to a depth of over 70 meters, and you're likely to see large pelagic fish passing by.

In the more southerly part of Shabrur Umm Gamar, along the eastern slope at a depth of between 25 and 40 meters, you'll find the remains of an Egyptian military ship. The ship does not merit close exploration because the hull is completely deteriorated and lacking any marks that could identify it. Nevertheless, the various species of sessile creatures that have covered the decayed wreckage are extremely interesting. However, beware of the possible presence of a deadly, skillfully camouflaged stonefish. A splendid giant grouper who is practically a permanent resident in this area of the reef often proves to be quite confident around divers.

As you proceed along the eastern slope, you'll notice that the wall inclines more at the point where the

reef is most exposed to the current. There is a large number of fish in this area. As you continue to swim northward, with the reef to your left, you'll come to an especially rich coral environment, particularly in the morning when it's completely illuminated by the sun. At this point, Shabrur Umm Gamar reef flaunts all its gorgeous colors and life teems around the large coral formations, which include fire coral (Millepora

dichotoma) and large brain corals.

From this point, rise slowly to shallower water, change direction, and keeping the reef on your right, return to the mooring area. Up to 15 meters from the surface, the entire Shabrur Umm Gamar reef is a succession of deep fissures full of coral fish and covered with a myriad of soft corals.

Paying attention to the numerous vertical cracks in the reef, in the shadows illuminated by a few shafts

D

E

of light you'll see timid lunartails (*Variola louti*) steephead parrotfish (*Lutjanus gibbus*), while near the wall are large humphead wrasses (*Cheilinus undulatus*) who swim after divers, attracted by the bubbles from their tanks. In the deep blue depths, you'll often see pelagic fish passing by, like tunas, bigeye trevallies (*Caranx sexfasciatus*), twinspot snapper (*Lutjanus bohar*) and sometimes gray sharks.

When you reach the southern edge of the reef, you'll find the mooring area, easily identifiable by the white sand floor.

G – If you look closely among the alcyonarian formations, you may see various species of animals hidden among the branches of these corals. It's common to see small brittle stars, crustaceans or cowries, such as Phenacovolva brevirostris.

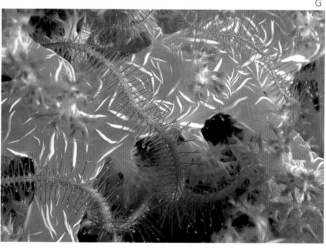

Careless Reef

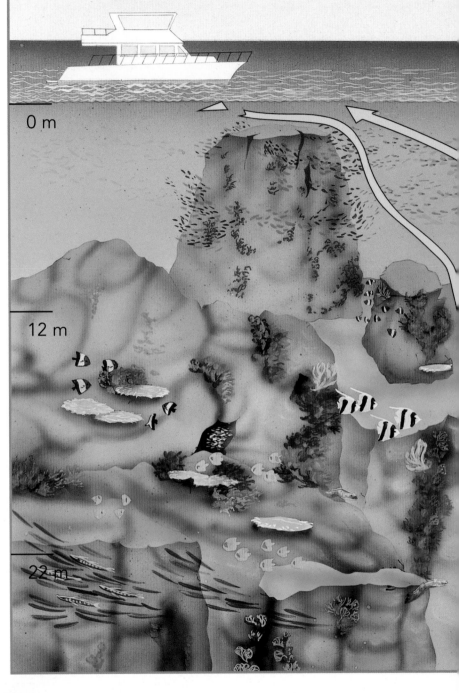

T HIS DIVING AREA consists of a vast submerged coral reef. The only points that reach the surface are two splendid towers a few dozen meters apart, connected by a wide coral saddle. The seabed from which the towers rise, with the northern tower the largest, forms a coral plateau with a depth that varies from 12 to 20 meters. South of the two pinnacles are the mooring buoys anchored on the floor of the reef. As the top reef is a few meters below the surface, the barrier does not offer boats safe shelter, especially when a strong north wind is blowing. For this reason, dives on Careless Reef are organized only when the weather and sea conditions are optimal. At Careless Reef, you can choose two different diving itineraries, depending on the current. The classic itinerary begins with a dive from the south side of the larger tower, near the boat mooring area. Once you've reached

the sea floor, 12 meters deep, go around the wall of the tower, keeping it on your right, until you come to the east side. Following the plateau for a few dozen meters, you'll come to the slope, where the reef begins to drop off into the abyss.

At a depth of 22 meters, the first pinnacle becomes clearly visible. At its base is a small cave that contains an incredible quantity of glassfish

A

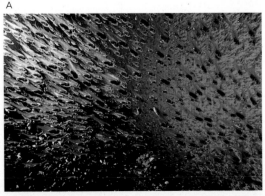

A – Glassfish (Parapriacanthus guentheri) are nocturnal creatures. During the day, they remain within caves or the dark recesses of shipwrecks.

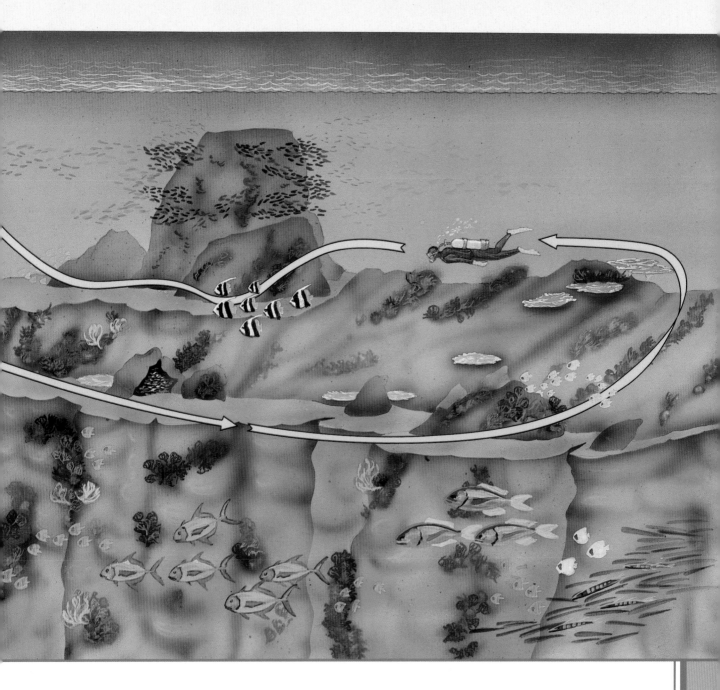

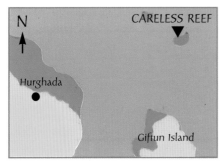

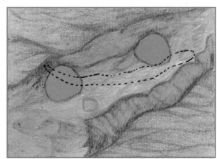

A – The yellowsaddle goatfish (Parapeneus cyclostomus) may be yellowish-gray with blue shading on each scale and a prominent yellow saddle-shaped spot on the caudal peduncle.

B – The Subergorgia hicksoni gorgonian, whose fans may be over two meters in size, is the largest and most spectacular gorgonian in the Red Sea. Its large branches may create a foundation for the growth of sea creatures such as the alcyonarians shown.

swimming in harmony among the narrow branches of the gorgonians. Remember to glance out to the open sea occasionally, where you may see schools of Suez fusiliers (Caesio suevicus), which quickly open up to make way for trevallies. You can also spot whitetip reef sharks (Triaenodon obesus) swimming tranquilly near the reef, especially in the morning, when the still weak sunlight creates an extremely evocative atmosphere.

Continuing your exploration of the wall amidst towers and gorgonians, you'll come to the northern tip of the reef, with a coral environment especially abundant in crevices and coral formations, all covered with alcyonarians and large sea fans

(*Subergorgia hicksoni*). From here, go back up to the coral terrace at a depth of 20 meters.

Following this stretch of plateau south, among the countless coral formations, you will see a splendid sampler of typical Red Sea fish: dense schools of pennantfish (*Heniochus intermedius*) rest peacefully in the shadow of Acropora corals, sharing their shelter with numerous blackspotted grunts (*Plectorhinchus gaterinus*), whose magnificent colors make them perfect subjects for photographs.

This area's main attraction, which has made Careless Reef famous among divers all over the world, is the giant morays (*Gymnothorax javanicus*) who find shelter in every crevice. In fact, it's

D

not uncommon to see them swimming along the sea floor in search of food or a new shelter.

Their innate meekness has always made them easy for divers to approach, and even today these morays have biological characteristics that are difficult to find in other areas of the Red Sea. But never forget that they are predators, and always be cautious and respectful when approaching them.

Unfortunately, for a number of years the crown-of-thorns starfish (*Acanthaster planci*) has been on the increase, leaving its indelible effects on the corals.

Continuing to swim south, you'll find the walls of the tower where the boat is moored.

C – Schools of trevallies can be seen along the walls of steep reefs plunging into the open sea, which make an excellent hunting ground for these silvery fish.

D – The blackspotted grunts (*Plectorhinchus gaterinus*) lives in small schools that by day can be seen beneath Acropora corals or within crevices.

E - The crown-of-thorns starfish (*Acanthaster planci*) is sadly famous as a destroyer of corals. It feeds primarily on coral polyps.

E

F

F – Alcyonarians come in a great variety of colors, from violet to deep red, and yellowish white to pale blue. They prefer reefs exposed to the current, which guarantees a constant inflow of food.

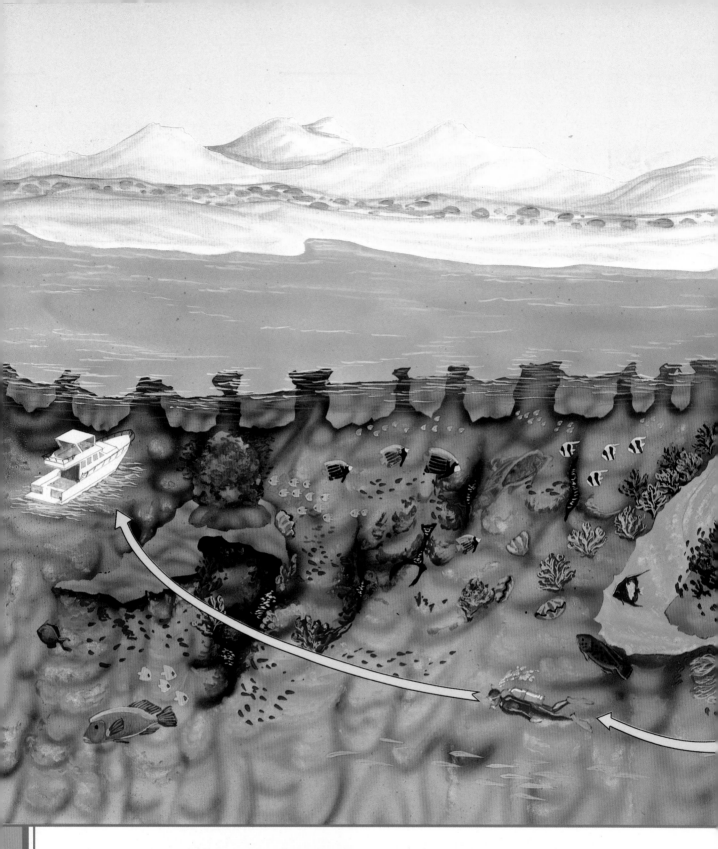

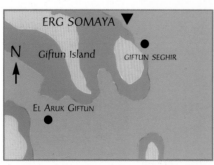

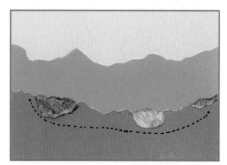

ERG SOMAYA ▼

N

Giftun Island

GIFTUN SEGHIR

EL ARUK GIFTUN

Erg Somaya

Depth markers:
0 m
18 m
22 m

A – The anemone coral attacks other corals by secreting toxic substances, allowing it to take over new territory.

B – When diving, it's important to be very careful of your position, or you may cause corals irreparable harm.

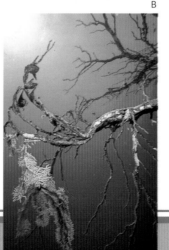

A

B

SAILING NORTH along the eastern wall of the island of Giftun Seghira, past its small lighthouse, you'll come to the diving area known as Erg Somaya, with two splendid coral towers and an especially lovely wall with a wealth of small recesses and several unique caves.

The mooring buoys, located in the shelter of the south tower, are the arrival point for this dive, which due to its characteristics should be made directly from a moving boat. If the sea is particularly rough, the boats will stay in a sheltered area to give all divers the chance to change, and will then head to the small inlet off the coast, where you'll enter the water. Following the reef from north to south with the current carrying you, you'll see a lively coral wall below you, full of countless crevices. The most interesting is a small grotto located at a depth of 30 meters, its entry framed by large branches of black coral and various species of stony corals. Illuminating the interior of the cave, you'll see lionfish completely surrounded by a myriad of glassfish. As they rapidly change directions, you can catch glimpses of slow *Pterois volitans* hovering motionless in the water. Following the wall south, with the reef to your right, go past a vast, sandy gully and climb the plateau to the first pinnacle. From a depth of 18 meters, it rises vertically toward the surface. The entire tower is covered with various species of majestic Acropora corals,

A

B

creating a delicate lacework around it. Schools of coral fish enliven this coral garden with their gaudy colors, while giant clams, well-protected within their sturdy, secure valves hidden among the corals, show off their gorgeous blues and greens.

Continuing the dive with the wall to your right, you'll see the second pinnacle at a depth of 22 meters. It has a unique pyramid structure with sides covered in broad sea fans (*Subergorgia hicksoni*), black corals, and alcyonarians reaching out to the open sea.

A multitude of coral fish populates the waters of Erg Somaya: schools of snappers, bright yellowsaddle goatfish (*Parupeneus cyclostomus*), yellowbar angelfish (*Pomacanthus maculosus*), blackspotted grunts (*Plectorhinchus gaterinus*), and wrasses fill every crevice of the reef with life.

Another interesting characteristic of these waters is the splendid chimney cave extending vertically along the outside drop-off of the reef not far from the second tower. Its openings are visible at 22 and 30 meters. Illuminating the interior of the tunnel, being very careful not to strike the delicate organisms growing in the dark cavity, you can admire lionfish (*Pterois volitans*), coral groupers (*Cephalopolis miniata*), and schools of *Parapriacanthus guentheri*.

During your dive, take a look out to the open sea occasionally, as this wall, dropping vertically for over 70

A – It's not uncommon to see bigeye trevallies (Caranx sexfasciatus) swimming alongside other species of fish. This photo shows a trevally and a lunertail grouper (Variola louti) swimming together.

B – Like most members of the Pomacanthidae family, yellowbar angelfish (Pomacanthus maculosus) can produce low frequency sounds similar to thuds. When larger individuals make these sounds, they are perfectly audible to divers as well.

C – Barracudas, which can be over one meter long, are formidable predators. They continuously patrol their territory in splendid schools that may contain hundreds of individuals.

D – The bluefin trevallies (Caranx melampygus) and Caranx sexfasciatus are some of the most common pelagic fish along the reefs of Hurghada. As they dart along the walls of the reefs, they create fantastic silver whirls of light and reflections.

E – Gorgonians can have different structures, from classic fan shapes to large, colorful tufts with long, flexible branches rising toward the surface.

F – The lionfish (Pterois volitans) is quite common along the coral reef throughout the Red Sea. With its large pectoral and dorsal fins, it is one of the most elegant fish in these waters.

meters, is an ideal place to see various kinds of pelagic fish, such as bigeye trevallies (*Caranx sexfasciatus*), barracudas (*Sphyraena barracuda*), and even a few sharks.

After admiring the various natural sights, ascend along the wall of the main reef, where you'll find the mooring buoy with the diving center boat that awaits you.

Giftun Seghir

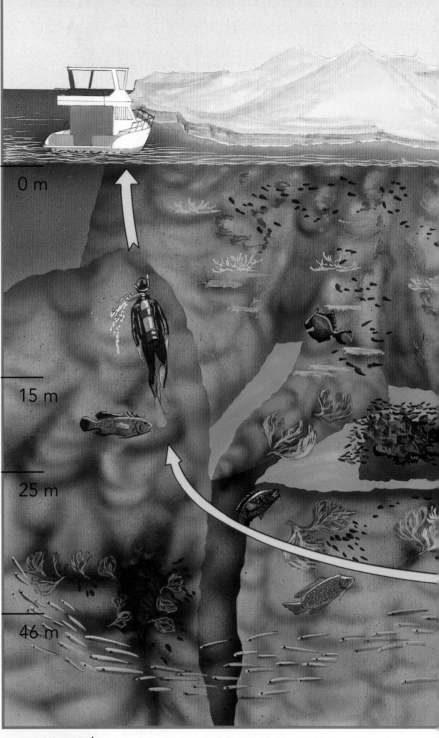

0 m

15 m

25 m

46 m

A

THE ISLAND OF GIFTUN SEGHIR is the smaller of the two Giftun Islands, located not far off the coast of Hurghada.

A dive along the east wall of the small island will reveal one of the most spectacular areas off Hurghada, located along a steep coral reef that plunges vertically off into the abyss. To reach your starting point, follow the island's eastern coast, and once you've identified a military antenna located in the shelter of the coast, go past it for a short distance to a small inlet. This is exactly where you should dive. The diving center boat will not moor in this rather windy area, but will tie to the buoys located to the south, where the coast forms a sheltered lee where your dive will end.

The best time to dive is mid-morning, when the sunlight fully illuminates the entire wall and lights up the colors of the reef.

Once in the water, go to the lee of the reef to begin your descent, and follow the current, which may be quite powerful on some days, keeping the reef on your right. With the current carrying you, the dive is a relaxing exploration along a magnificent wall, where you can "fly over" extensive stretches of black coral (*Cirripathes anguina*) and large sea fans (*Subergorgia hicksoni*) whose beauty has given this area the name Gorgonia Reef.

During the whole dive, keep an

A – The pure white beach of Mahmya has become a mandatory stop during daily excursions from Hurghada. You can eat excellent fish at the perfectly designed local restaurant.

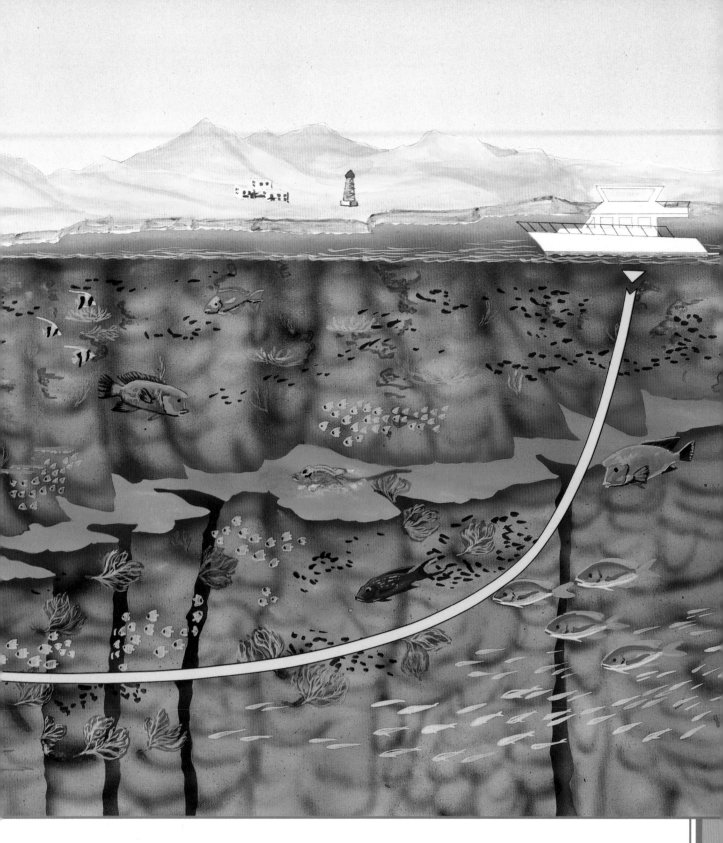

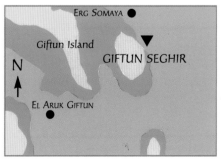

ERG SOMAYA ●

Giftun Island

▼

GIFTUN SEGHIR

N

El Aruk Giftun ●

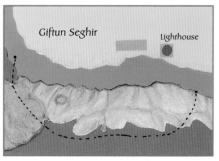

Giftun Seghir

Lighthouse

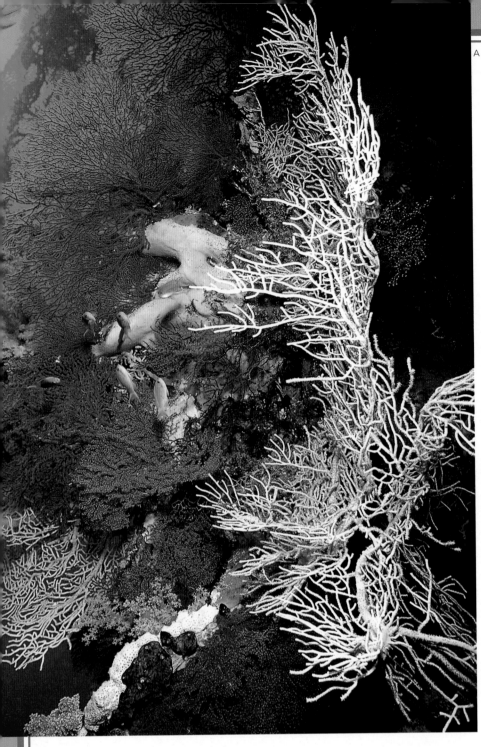

A

A – The various species of gorgonians that grow in the Red Sea live primarily along reef walls that drop vertically into the blue depths, or near tunnel caves, where the current's flow grows more powerful, bringing in more nourishment.

B – The waters of the Red Sea contain various species of sea turtles, the most numerous of which is Eretmochelis imbricata, which can reach up to a meter in length.

C

balance of sessile fauna that covers the coral rocks. After passing the cave, ascend to a shallower depth and then once again follow the main wall of the reef, which at this point separates into two large branches. To the south, the wall leads outwards, while if you follow it to the southwest, it will lead you to a wide sandy terrace at a depth of 25 to 10 meters and a base with

eye on the open sea, where it's not uncommon to see various pelagic fish such as tunas, trevallies and even solitary hammerhead sharks (*Sphyrna lewini*). In a few minutes you'll come to a massive coral spit that forms a sort of underwater promontory. Here, at a depth of 46 meters, you'll find a spectacular tunnel cave. Using a good flashlight, you can see small yellow gorgonians covering the walls inside it, coral groupers (*Cephalopholis miniata*) and large redmouth groupers (*Aethaloperca rogaa*).

Don't go too far in, or you may damage the extremely fragile

B

D

C – The bluespotted lagoon ray (Taeniura lymna) has a discoid body with a tapered tail, armed at the tip with two sturdy saw-toothed spines, which can inflict deep wounds on aggressors in case of danger.

D – The small twobar anemonefish (Amphiprion bicinctus) can be seen in pairs or small groups, always among the tentacles of various anemones, such as (Entacmaea quadricolor) and Heteractis magnifica.

E – The stony coral (Turbinaria mesenterina) forms vertical plates with volutes of a characteristic yellowish color. During the night, the polyps extend their tentacles outward in order to capture particles of food.

F – The yellowish-green broccoli coral (Lythophyton arboreum) belongs to the large family of soft corals. Their ability to live in sediment-rich environments helps them in the fierce competition for territory along the walls of the reef.

numerous coral formations. Here, it's common to see large sea turtles (Chelonia mydas) and porcupinefish, usually hidden under the broad Acropora umbrellas. Another curious aspect of these waters can be discovered if you carefully observe the sandy areas alternating with the corals, where you can spot the mimetic colors of crocodilefish, spotted stingrays, and a few almost invisible little sole (Pardachirus marmoratus).

In the shelter of the reef, a large school of yellowtail goatfish oscillates in a compact mass between the base of the reef and the underlying coral formations.

Not far from the boat mooring area, a friendly family of humphead wrasses (Cheilinus undulatus) awaits divers, ready to give them the final surprise of this marvelous dive.

Accompanied by these sociable, amusing creatures, you'll come to the mooring buoys area.

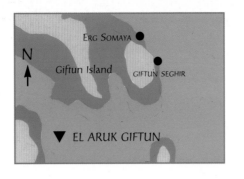

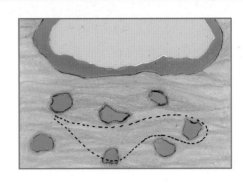

A – The bluespotted lagoon ray (Taeniura lymna) hunts invertebrates and crustaceans by uncovering them from the sandy sea floor.

B – Clownfish (Amphiprion bicinctus) rub against the mucus covering the anemone to impregnate themselves and become "invisible" to the sensors of the poisonous cells.

A

B

El Aruk Giftun

0 m

12 m

EL ARUK GIFTUN is a very special diving area, consisting of a sandy floor 12 meters deep with coral blocks rising from the bottom to the water's surface. Sheltered by the island of Giftun Kebir, they are well-protected from the wind.

Not far from the island of Giftun Kebir, to the north of Gotha Abu Ramada, El Aruk is about a half hour's sail from Hurghada.

Near the main towers that comprise El Aruk Giftun are various mooring buoys that provide a safe anchoring site for boats from diving centers, which find this an ideal place to organize a second dive.

Your descent into the water begins directly from the boat's mooring site. Once you've reached the bottom, be sure to completely memorize the route you take among the towers, so you won't become disoriented and have trouble finding your way back to the boat. Although some of these coral columns are rather far apart, with brief sandy stretches you must cross to reach them, your dive will still be interesting and pleasant due to the shallow depth and the sunlight reflecting on the white sand floor.

In the center of this vast area, formed of numerous coral columns,

A

their anemones, bluespotted lagoon rays, crocodilefish camouflaged in the sand, and a thousand other players in this underwater theater. Despite the shallow depth, which makes the dive extremely easy, you may encounter currents of average strength that could make the dive a little more difficult. Moving through these corals is like swimming in a magical aquarium that almost miraculously includes most of the creatures that live around the reef.

Splendid corals are home to various species in the Serranidae family, from small blackspotted groupers (*Epinephelus fasciatus*), to large, cunning spotted groupers (*Plectropomus pessuliferus*), while swirls of wrasses alternate with the vivid colors of masked butterflyfish

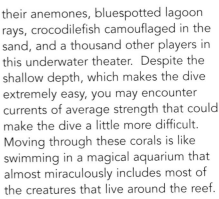

C

you'll find one that is much bigger than the others, with a spectacular tunnel cave. Usually, in the shadows of this underwater tunnel you can see numerous lionfish (*Pterois volitans*, clouds of glassfish (*Parapriacanthus guentheri*), and small red groupers (*Cephalopholis hemistiktos*).

A dive into the coral maze of El Aruk Giftun is relatively simple, but certainly no less interesting than other seabeds. The area is highly recommended for photography buffs, who will find excellent subjects for fabulous photos: schools of immobile butterflyfish, clownfish enveloped in

B

D

A – To make newly hatched twobar anemonefish (Amphiprion bicinctus) *immune to the anemone's poison, the parents rub a few tentacles against the eggs deposited at the base of the* anemone, so that the mucus covers the eggs and immunizes the embryo.

B – The almost transparent structure of alcyonarians makes it possible to observe the numerous calcareous spicules that make the animal's structure more robust.

E

(*Chaetodon semilarvatus*), which in their turn seem to be chasing after large angelfish (*Pomacanthus maculosus*).

During your exploration of these coral columns, don't focus only on the base of the pinnacles, but look at the walls as well, where the sunlight sets off the variety of colors of the various species of corals, like the violet raspberry coral (*Pocillopora verrucosa*), green brain coral (*Favia favus*), or yellow *Tubinaria mesenterina*.

Even the sandy areas that separate the towers have their secrets. In fact, it's not uncommon to see devilfish (*Inimicus filamentosus*) half-hidden in the sand, along with thin pipefish (*Corythoichthys schultzi*) and skillfully camouflaged reef lizardfish (*Saurida gracilis*).

You could spend hours admiring the extraordinary spectacle nature offers, if it weren't for the pressure gauge jolting you back to reality!

C – *Large branches of extraordinarily colorful alcyonarians grow in the darkness of caves, the preferred refuge for silvery schools of glassfish (*Parapriacanthus guentheri*).*

D – *Sea cucumbers, echinoderms with a cylindrical body, feed on organic detritus that they swallow as they crawl along the sea floor. Their mouths are almost always surrounded by small tentacles, which they use to capture particles of food.*

E – *The devilfish (*Inimicus filamentosus*) uses its lower pectoral fins like little feet to "walk" along the sandy floors. Sometimes one can be seen completely buried in sediments, only its eyes protruding.*

F – *The wealth of color that the Red Sea offers, even at just a few meters deep, has made this sea one of the world's most famous and desirable destinations for divers.*

F

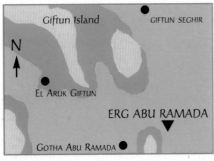

Erg Abu Ramada

T HE ERG ABU RAMADA DIVING AREA, located in the shelter of the island of the same name, is about a 30 minute sail from the coast of Hurghada and is located a few kilometers south of Giftun Island.

The waters where you'll be taking your dive are located around three coral towers, in Arabic known as "erg," to the southeast of the island of Abu Ramada. The buoys used to moor the boats are south of the largest tower, not far from the reef. As this area is especially exposed to north winds, it's not always possible to dive here, because there is no truly sheltered area. Your dive will begin directly from the boat mooring area. Thus, once in the water, if a strong current is running in the other direction, you should quickly get to the base of the

0 m

5 m

13 m

20 m

A

A – If touched, gorgonian polyps can quickly dilate and contract their eight tentacles.

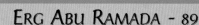

plateau at 18 meters deep, trying to use the coral walls of the tower as a shelter to aid your movements. The underwater currents that sweep this area are an important source of energy for the underwater world, as they carry in large amounts of food that permit more robust development of the sessile fauna on the reef.

The diving itinerary winds through this maze of three coral towers with a base about 20 meters deep. You'll discover passages opening among the coral walls, where you can admire a surprising abundance of life. On the east side of the first tower, you'll find several crevices in the rock completely covered with colorful alcyonarians, which look especially turgid in the current.

After carefully exploring the largest of the three *erg*, go to the second and then the third. Take advantage of the shallow depth to examine the numerous pinnacles.

A - *Small scalefin anthias* (Pseudanthias squamipinnis) *can be seen only by day. At night, they hide in the crevices of the reef.*

B – Pseudanthias taeniatus, *red with a prominent white band, frequents the same coral environments as scalefin anthias* (Pseudanthias squamipinnis).

While at first they may look alike, they actually have very different characteristics. You can admire other caves whose shadowy depths reveal gorgonians and soft corals, with schools of transparent glassfish (*Parapriacanthus guentheri*) swimming through their branches.

Entire stretches of reef are colonized by large alcyonarians and gorgonians, which enliven the reef with their brilliant colors. Every crevice hides red groupers, splendid

D

C - The giant
moray
(Gymnothorax
javanicus) is a
formidable
nocturnal predator:
during the day, it
hides among the
corals as it waits for
prey to pass by.

E

*D – The graceful
beauty of the
lionfish (Pterois
volitans) makes
these animals one
of the most sought-
after subjects for
underwater
photography.*

*E – The pink or
violet color of
sponges is caused
by several species
of symbiotic algae
present within their
structures.*

morays, schools of sweetlips, and
many other species of coral fish.
During your dive, you may also meet
two especially friendly families of
humphead wrasses (Chelinus
undulatus). Rotating their eyes 360°,
they'll approach to watch curiously
everything happening around them.

A quick exploration of the base of
the reef to the east, where the floor
descends to depths of over 30
meters, will show a continuous
succession of coral walls and vast
sandy plateaus from which rise red
whip corals (Juncella juncea), easily
identifiable by their threadlike form
with absolutely no branches. If you
carefully look at the base of these
corals, you'll see the small, mimetic
dwarf coral goby (Bryaninops
youngei).

Before ending your dive, after
returning to the largest erg, where
the boats moor, carefully explore the
upper area of the towers as well,
which is populated by small sea
creatures that are too often ignored.
You'll see a myriad of anthias whose
bright scales and sudden darting
movements fill every crevice of the
reef with color.

Don't miss a dive at Erg Abu
Ramada during your stay at
Hurghada, because the life teeming
around these towers is truly
extraordinary.

A

B

A – The coral grouper is a formidable predator. Hidden among the corals, it captures small fish in lightning attacks.

B – The masked butterflyfish (Chaetodon semilarvatus) is active by day. At night, its color grows darker as it takes refuge among the corals.

Gotha Abu Ramada

ONE OF THE MOST FASCINATING DIVES in the waters of Hurghada is at Gotha Abu Ramada, an oval-shaped reef two miles south of the island of Abu Ramada. The area is commonly known as "Aquarium" due to the wealth of coral life, which allows divers to explore a vast range of coral fish from a wide variety of species.

Diving center boats moor on the south side, where there are various buoys fixed to a sandy bottom about 12 meters deep.

Several coral towers rise around the main reef, which consists of an extensive coral barrier that ends on a sandy floor between 12 and 18 meters deep. These towers form a crown around the entire coastal perimeter of Gotha Abu Ramada.

From the southern side, where the boats moor, you can follow two different diving itineraries: one heading

12 m

18 m

Giftun Island

GIFTUN SEGHIR

N

EL ARUK GIFTUN

ERG ABU RAMADA

GOTHA ABU RAMADA ▼

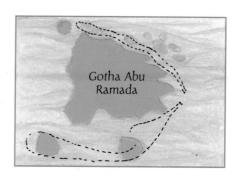

Gotha Abu Ramada

A – The twobar
anemonefish
(Amphiprion
bicinctus) *never
goes far from its
anemone, which
guarantees it
shelter from
possible predators.*

A

B – A school of
masked
butterflyfish swims
over a sandy sea
floor, where the
profile of a
crocodile fish
(cociella crocodila)
is visible.

C – Schools of
blackspotted
grunts
(Plectorhinchus
gaterinus) are
always a fascinating
sight. Lazily
tranquil, they will
fearlessly allow
divers to come
quite close.

B

east and one west.

The eastern itinerary follows the reef from the left side, until you reach a series of massive coral formations rising up not far from the reef. As you explore the life forms around these towers, you'll find it easy to see why Gotha Abu Ramada reef is known as "Aquarium."

Dense schools of scalefin anthias (Pseudanthias squamipinnis), blackspotted grunts (Plectorhinchus gaterinus), twinspot snapper (Lutjanus bohar), blackspot snapper s (Lutjanus ehrenbergi), and other varieties of

sedentary fish find shelter among the coral branches. If you explore the sandy floor, you'll find bluespotted lagoon rays (Taeniura lymna), crocodilefish (cociella crocodila) and graceful gobies.

Continuing your dive while keeping the main reef to your left, you'll come to two more coral towers, which host schools of yellowfin goatfish (Mulloides vanicolensis), musked butterflyfish (Chaetodon semilarvatus), and numerous brightly colored wrasses surrounding the walls of this reef. After lingering to explore these blocks, continue along the reef, or else slowly

return, changing direction and this time keeping the wall to your right.

The second itinerary always begins on the south side of Gotha where, keeping the coral reef to the right, you proceed along the west side of the main reef until you reach the western tip. Here, about 50 meters from the reef, are two large coral blocks with numerous crevices that serve as dens for morays and groupers. The outer walls of these coral formations are covered with the gorgeous colors of gorgonians and soft corals.

The most interesting area is the

northernmost tower. A friendly family of lionfish *(Pterois volitans)* lives among the crevices and will fearlessly come out of their shelters to swim in the open water.

Continuing the dive along the main wall of the reef, you'll reach the side facing the northwest, where you'll see ever-present schools of cornetfish *(Fistularia commersonii)*, empero angelfish *(Pomacanthus imperator)* and goatfish. In the summer are quite numerous titan triggerfish *(Balistoides viridescens)* and blue yellow spotted triggerfish *(Pseudobalistes fuscus)*, which you can see intent on moving tiny blocks of coral and sand with their mouths to create little holes in the sea floor, where the females will later deposit their eggs.

Even the most demanding divers will find that dives at Gotha Abu Ramada make them feel like they're swimming in a marvelous natural aquarium.

D – Groups of lionfish (Pterois volitans) *are common in some parts of the reef,* where they can be seen using their large fins to hover in the crystalline water.

E – The yellowfin goatfish (Mulloides vanicolensis) *is the only goatfish to live in schools of over 100 individuals. It frequents shallower zones of the reef, in the shelter of coral formations.*

Makadi Bay

0 m

15 m

SOUTH OF THE TOWN OF HURGHADA, across from the new Makadi tourist center, is a coral reef that still has extremely interesting natural features. Until just a few years ago, one could see shy, majestic manatees in this area, who came to the tranquil bays in search of food. Today, much has changed, and it's increasingly difficult to find pristine bays like Makadi.

Due to the shallow water and lack of a current, this entire reef area is also excellent for snorkelers.

The dive begins near the coastal reef, where, once you've entered the water, you should follow the reef to the sandy bottom that gently descends from a depth of 15 meters out toward the open sea. Here there are numerous coral pinnacles that provide shelter to various communities of coral fish. The upper portion of the reef is lively and spectacular. Schools of coral fish hover in the intricate maze of corals.

The infinite variety of forms and species includes small hurnbug dascyllus (*Dascyllus aruanus*), white with black bands, pennantfish (*Heniochus intermedius*), and *Chromis viridis* that flee into the corals at the slightest provocation. If you're attentive, you may glimpse a tiny, graceful, brilliant violet olive dottyback (*Pseudochromis fridmani*), one of the fish endemic to the Red Sea. Continuing your dive,

A

A – The redtooth triggerfish (Odonus niger), with its beautiful blue color and falcate tail, lives in large schools near the reef. If it feels threatened, it flees to the nearest crack, with only the loves of its caudal fin protruding.

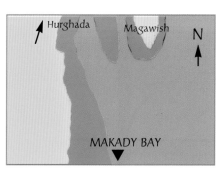

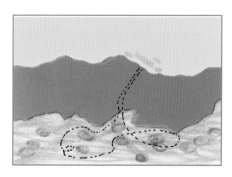

A

A – The crocodile fish (cociella crocodila) is territorial, and likes to remain motionless in the sand as it awaits small prey, which it captures by sucking it into its wide, gaping mouth.

B – Four things must happen for a reef to form: a colony of stony corals must develop, colonies must join to form a single unit, sedimentation must occur to fill in the spaces among the colonies, and they must be cemented into a single calcareous bank.

C – The flexibility of red gorgonians (Melithaea sp.) is due to breaks in the axial structure, which consists of spicules that are not fused together, but connected by a horny material that allows the branches to oscillate and bend with the current.

E – Corals with bulky structures are the primary contributors to reef construction, while those with branched forms are a secondary element to the growth of the bank and the formation of coral sand.

F – A brightly colored mollusk moves among the branches of an alcyonarian, which displays its expanded polyps. Despite their vulnerability, sea slugs are poisonous to many fish, as their brilliant colors warn.

B

C

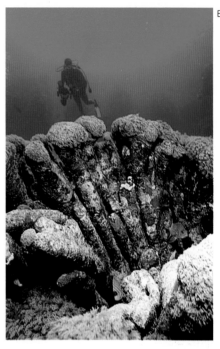

E

you'll reach the base of the reef, where you'll find a more varied, complex environment teeming with life and color, especially around midday, when it's totally illuminated by the sun.

Spend most of your time exploring this broad plateau, where tall coral pinnacles alternate with areas of white sand, creating a varied, especially lovely seascape that will give photographers the chance to take some unusual shots. The tops of the coral formations,

which rise solitary from the sandy bottom, are surrounded by schools of Suez fusiliers (Caesio suevicus) that create marvelous whirls of silver.

The luminous environment and transparent water help set off this surprisingly spectacular underwater garden, constantly traversed by surgeonfish, twinspot snapper (Lutjanus bohar), blackspot snappers (Lutjanus ehrenbergi), and even a few large, solitary barracudas, hovering immobile

in the water as they wait to seize some unwary prey.

During your dive, don't forget to carefully observe the sandy areas in the shelter of the corals, where, you can spot well-camouflaged crocodilefish (Cociella crocodila), large stingrays hidden below the rocks, covered with a thin layer of sand, bluespotted lagoon stingrays (Taeniura lymna), and various types of gobies; it's not even uncommon to see stonefish (Synanceia verrucosa), their spines concealing a powerful poison.

While there's no precise, set itinerary to follow, once you've finished your exploration of this coral labyrinth, head to the wall of the main reef, where, rising to the surface, you will find several small caves that provide shelter for schools of glassfish (Parapriacanthus guentheri).

The floor of Makadi Bay, shallow and full of life and color, is a place where you could spend hours watching the extraordinary spectacle nature offers you, but sooner or later you'll have to come back up!

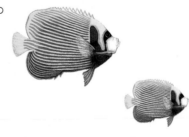

D

D – In some tunnel caves, constant flows of currents are created that form an ideal habitat for the development of various sessile species like alcyonarians and gorgonians. It's not uncommon to see a great variety of fish within these tunnels.

Safaga

THE CITY OF SAFAGA, located about 60 kilometers south of Hurghada, has changed greatly over recent years as a result of the sharp increase in tourism in the mid-1990's, which had a great impact on its economy. Until recently, Safaga was the largest Egyptian port on the coast of the western Red Sea. In addition to being the point of departure for thousands of pilgrims headed for Mecca via sea, its economy was based primarily on mining and exporting phosphates. Today, Safaga can be considered

one of the most important tourist towns on the Egyptian coast, right after Hurghada and Sharm el Sheikh.

A splendid district known as Soma Bay was recently opened within the bay of Ras Abu Soma, a little less than 10 kilometers north of Safaga. It includes four world renowned hotels, including the Sheraton Soma Bay, with a Diving World scuba diving center. In the center of the peninsula is Soma Bay's Golf and Country Club, a magnificent 18 hole golf course with a spectacular panoramic view of the sea.

Proceeding along the main road past Ras Abu Soma, before reaching the town, you'll find the village area two kilometers north of Safaga.

The rapid transformation over recent years was certainly facilitated by the beauty of the coast, which opens out into a vast gulf between the tip of Ras Abu Soma, to the north, and a wide coral reef that borders the cove to the south. The coast is a splendid succession of long beaches that crown the reef and small islands that conceal still pristine waters with a wealth of secrets to discover.

You can explore countless diving areas during your stay at Safaga. These areas can be divided into two distinct zones, based on their position.

The area closest to the coast, included between the promontory of Ras Abu Soma and the northern tip of Safaga Island, has a series of relatively shallow reefs. It offers numerous diving areas at Tobya and Gamul, which are completely sheltered from the north wind and always offer diving possibilities regardless of sea conditions. The second diving area is in the open sea, over an hour's sail away, where there is an underwater ridge with various reefs whose splendid coral walls plunge vertically into the abyss. The most representative diving areas in this part of the sea are Panorama Reef, Sha'ab Sheer, and Abu Kefan. As these areas are quite rough and swept by powerful currents, they are not always accessible to diving boats.

The waters of a small reef located near Sha'ab Sheer conceals the hull of the *Salem Express*, a ferry that sank in the night between December 15-16, 1991, taking the lives of hundreds of pilgrims from Mecca. Another natural feature that is a key to Safaga's fame and success is the desert mountains, whose tall peaks rising up near the sea create a scene of magnificent beauty. These mountains hold interesting archaeological sites, including the remains of the Roman city of *Mons Claudianus*, in Arabic "Umm Digal," or the "Mother of

A – A sailing vessel along the coast of Safaga, where rosy mountains merge with the transparent waters, creating a dreamlike backdrop.

B – Close-up of an enormous block of granite the Romans once used to build columns for the great palaces of Rome. In the background, the remains of the city of Mons Claudianus, *located near a quarry that produced this valuable mineral.*

C – The sea anemone (Heteractis magnifica) adheres to coral using its stubby red body, which ends in an oral disk with innumerable greenish-yellow tentacles.

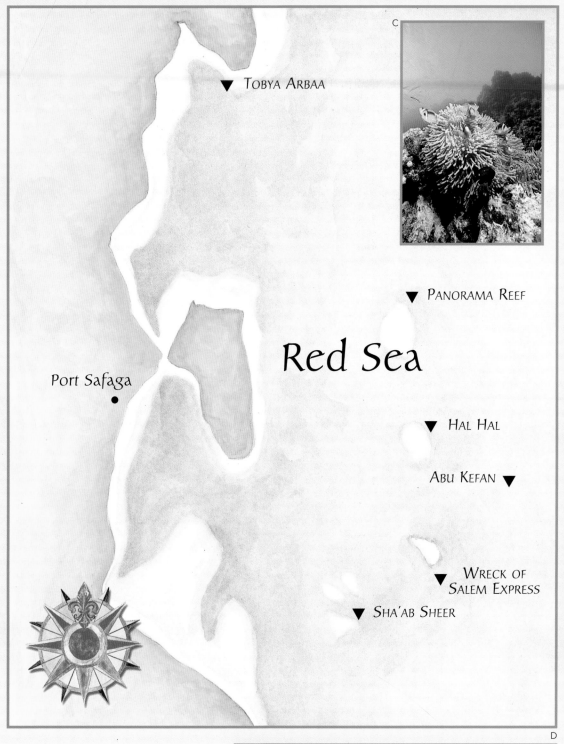

TOBYA ARBAA ▼

C

▼ PANORAMA REEF

Red Sea

Port Safaga
●

▼ HAL HAL

ABU KEFAN ▼

▼ WRECK OF SALEM EXPRESS

▼ SHA'AB SHEER

Columns." The name comes from ancient times, when precious granite was mined from this land and used to make the capitals of columns for important Roman buildings. If you visit the archaeological area, you can admire large mounds of pottery, amphorae, and several architectural works not yet completely removed from the mountain rock. Although Safaga is growing rapidly, outside the little town there are still vast stretches of desert, soon to be developed with luxurious hotels.

D – "The Cascades," a futuristic golf course, is part of the Soma Bay complex. The green grass contrasts with the bright blue sea and the golden desert behind it. Gary Player, one of the three greatest golfers of all times, designed this finely equipped golf course.

D

Tobya Arbaa

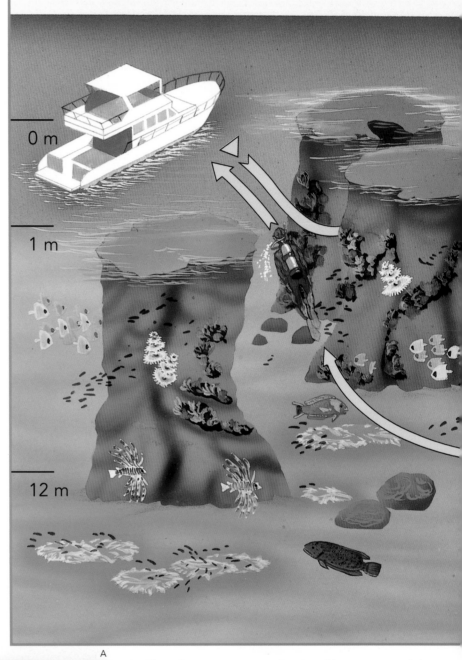

0 m

1 m

12 m

SOUTH OF THE BROAD PROMONTORY of Ras Abu Soma, seven coral pinnacles rise from a sandy floor 12 meters deep. Located below the coast, they are well protected from the north winds.

Four of these towers are especially large, and perhaps for this reason the area is known as "arbaa," which in Arabic means "four." The reefs of Tobya are quite interesting from the naturalistic perspective, and are especially thrilling at night. The spectacle these waters offer during a night dive is truly incomparable, as the marine fauna becomes amazingly active after sunset. At that time, in the dark, the coral reef dons its most gaudy garb, offering divers astounding sights.

Due to the weak current and shallow depth, you can easily explore this underwater world so full of surprises. You should carefully

A

A – The pajama slug (Chromodoris quadricolor) with its lovely yellow mantle and white and black stripes, covers the outer tissues of its small body with the calcareous or siliceous spicules it takes from the sponges on which it feeds.

memorize your itinerary around the coral towers so that you won't have difficulty finding the boat's mooring position when the dive is over.

As soon as you enter the water, follow the upper edge of the reef, where you'll see numerous crinoids at a few meters deep. Illuminated by your flashlight, they extend their feathery arms out into the dark, while the splendid *Astroboa nuda*

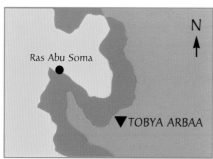

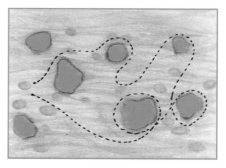

A

D

stars quickly retract their long tentacles, forming curious tangles.

All the towers are covered with colorful alcyonarians and small yellow gorgonians. Particularly showy are the coral polyps, which expand in the dark and swell their tiny crowns of tentacles in a constant search for food. Going deeper, your flashlight will reveal a myriad of small, phosphorescent points of light among the coral branches, and you'll see graceful *Stenopus hispidus* shrimp with their long, slender, pure white antennae.

If you're attentive, you may have one of the most unique encounters with nocturnal life in the Red Sea. Indeed, it won't be difficult to spot parrotfish who surround themselves with a sort of gelatinous cocoon before going to sleep, to prevent nocturnal predators from tracking their scent.

To observe these surprising aspects of nature, you should make your dive in complete darkness. The difference in behavior between diurnal and nocturnal creatures becomes evident at precise times, usually after sunset and a little before dawn. From every tower you'll see groups of lionfish *Pterois volitans* hovering immobile in the water. Unfazed by divers and attracted by the flashlight beams on the light sand, they take the opportunity to feast in the light, offering a unique spectacle.

You'll also frequently encounter *Hexabranchus sanguineus* nudibranchs, more commonly known as Spanish dancers, whose elegant, undulating movements and

B

A – Gorgonians grow from two to four centimeters a year, with a proportional increase in diameter. Their approximate age can be determined by counting the growth rings in the base.

B – The titan triggerfish (Balistoides viridescens) has strong teeth that allow it to eat even long-spined urchins.

C – Parrotfish owe their name to their unique teeth, which fit into a structure similar to a sturdy beak.

D – Gorgonian branches grow out to create a surface perpendicular to the flow of water, so the organism can more easily intercept food carried by the current.

C

refined red mantle are similar to flamenco dancers. Don't forget to explore the sandy areas among the reefs. With a little luck, you may see a turtle drowsing on the sea floor. Each tower hides a secret to be revealed by careful exploration. The towers may appear to be similar, but each little crevice actually contains the life of a small sea creature.

This dive is especially enjoyable for macrophotography enthusiasts, who will have fine opportunities for marvelous close-ups.

E - Cheilodipterus macrodon, *the tiger cardinal fish, owes its name to its sharp teeth like small fangs, which can be seen even when the fish's mouth is closed. It lives in caves or under the umbrella of Acropora corals.*

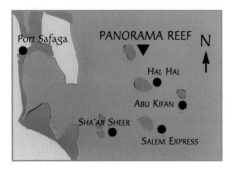

PANORAMA REEF N

Port Safaga

Hal Hal

Abu Kifan

Sha'ab Sheer

Salem Express

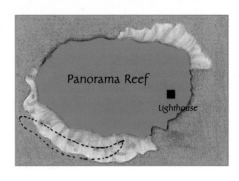

Panorama Reef

Lighthouse

A

A – The silvery flashes of light that schools of trevallies create in the blue depths of the open sea are doubtless one of the most spectacular, thrilling sights any diver could experience.

Panorama Reef

0 m

20 m

37 m

Panorama Reef is more than an hour's sail northeast of the port of Safaga. It is also known as Abu Alama, which in Arabic means "father of the pennant," due to a small lighthouse on the southwest point of the reef. It is one of the most spectacular diving areas on this coast. Panorama Reef is rounded, with two plateaus running northwest – southeast. The mooring buoys are set on the southern and western side of the reef, as these areas are especially sheltered from the wind and guarantee secure anchorage for boats.

As this is a vast coral shelf in the open sea, Panorama Reef provides various diving itineraries, which must always be planned after carefully evaluating the direction and intensity of the current.

The most interesting area is located along the eastern side of the reef. Drift diving is most common in this part of the reef, so that divers can begin their descent on the northern side of Panorama and then let the current carry them along the entire east wall until they come to the internal area of the reef, where the

A – The small tentacles of gorgonian polyps have stinging nematocysts used to immobilize their prey.

B – The largest anemonefish is always a female.

C – The humphead wrasse (Cheilinus undulatus) may weigh up to two hundred kilograms and measure nearly 3 meters in length.

D – Hidden within the large fans of gorgonians are sponges, mollusks and crustaceans.

E - Onespot snapper (Lutjanus monostigma) lives in small schools at the edge of the reef, where it is constantly in pursuit of fusiliers and other small prey.

mooring buoys are located.

As soon as you jump in, you'll see a spectacular drop-off plunging vertically into the deep blue sea, with an interruption at 37 meters, where the barrier forms a slight ledge, and then drops off once again into the abyss. The wall looks like an immense palette of color due to the abundant presence of corals, alcyonarians and sea fan (Subergorgia hicksoni), on which you can often see small longnose hawkfish (Oxycirrhites typus) and the endemic olive dottyback (Pseudochromis fridmani). Right at the edge of the drop-off, you'll see a forest of gigantic gorgonians, which have grown abnormally large due to their exposure to the current and are almost horizontal to the surface, creating a truly evocative pattern of light and shadow, especially for photographers.

As you explore the sides facing the open sea, you'll frequently encounter various species of pelagic fish, such as gray sharks, whitetip reef sharks (Triaenodon obesus), tunas and bigeye trevallies (Caranx sexfasciatus).

Before reaching the southeast tip where the boats are moored, rise slightly toward the surface, where, 20 meters deep, the wall of the reef creates a broad coral plateau full of Acropora corals and other stony coral formations, as well as various species of soft corals.

Currents are quite common as you move among the coral towers, so you need to watch your air consumption, even though the current itself is what aids the growth of coral, which feeds on the plankton it carries in.

When you round the south side of the wall, near the boat mooring area, you'll find a special point of this reef known as "Anemone City." It is an extraordinary concentration of red and violet anemones growing vertically along the wall of the reef, from 18 meters deep to nearly the surface. It almost seems a curious joke of nature, as it is difficult to find such a concentration of the same species of anemone in other areas. Hundreds of families of twobar anemonefish (Amphiprion bicinctus) find refuge within these anemones, often with their newborn, yet already territorial and aggressive offspring. It's an ideal place to end your dive on Panorama Reef before you come to the mooring buoys. Still, don't forget to look for yet another family of humphead wrasses (Cheilinus undulatus), who often hover under the keels.

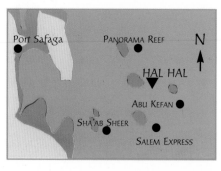

Port Safaga
Panorama Reef
N
HAL HAL
Abu Kefan
Sha'ab Sheer
Salem Express

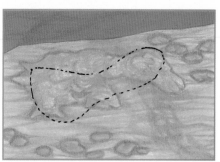

Hal Hal

5 m

16 m

25 m

T HE CORAL BLOCK OF HAL HAL is about a 2 hour sail from the coast of Safaga. The name fishermen gave this area means "place where the sea is always rough and foamy." Your dive will be around two large coral formations that are particularly exposed to waves and currents, which make it difficult to dive here on days when the wind is strong. When you reach the diving area, the boats will head to the tower to the north, where you'll dive in from the moving boat, which will then moor at the southern tower, where the anchoring buoys are located.

Before entering the water, carefully evaluate the intensity and direction of the current, which can be unpredictable and quite powerful in this area. When the waters of Hal Hal are swept by these currents, once in the water, you should quickly dive to the established depth and remain within the shelter of the wall as much as possible. This way, you can go against the current and more easily admire the extraordinary richness of the reef.

The currents so common in this area create ideal conditions for the growth of marine life, and help produce an extraordinarily lively reef, where the smallest coral is surrounded by clouds of fish with the most incredible forms and colors. The Hal Hal diving area is formed by two enormous coral blocks located close together, rising at the edge of a vast

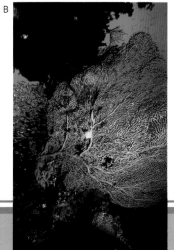

A – With its variegated color and numerous protuberances, the lionfish (Pterois volitans) can camouflage itself perfectly.

B – The large, fan-like tangled structures of the gorgonians are home to a fantastic array of small animals.

A

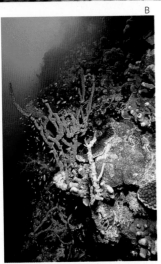

B

C

A – A school of pennantfish (Heniochus intermedius) *has established its territory among the contorted structures of large Acropora corals.*

B – The stony coral formations of this reef offer divers true explosions of color. Nourished by the current, splendid examples of alcyonarians, gorgonians and sponges live here.

coral plateau, creating a sharp drop-off toward the open sea. Between these two "loaves" is a coral saddle through which a powerful current flows. For this reason, its walls are covered with spectacular alcyonarians that are particularly rich in oxygen.

The side facing west has a coral wall that slopes down on the sand at about 16 meters deep. After a wide ledge at a depth of 25 meters, the eastern side drops vertically without interruption to over 80 meters deep. An enormous quantity of soft corals, gorgonians, alcyonarians and fish of every kind make Hal Hal a truly

C – Trevallies are a common sight along the outer walls of the reef, where they hunt in schools.

D – The exceptional transparency of the waters of the Red Sea enhances the incredible variety of colors that can be admired among the branches of these alcyonarians growing within a coral canyon.

E – The spotted grouper (Plectopomus pessuliferus), which may exceed one meter in length, is a formidable predator.

F – Like all pufferfish, the Arothron diadematus has the ability to swell up when it feels threatened. It rapidly pumps water into a highly extendible ventral diverticulum, which allows it to significantly increase the size of its body.

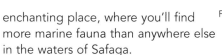

enchanting place, where you'll find more marine fauna than anywhere else in the waters of Safaga.

If you dive along these walls, you'll have the opportunity to encounter various species of sedentary fish. Under the broad umbrellas of Acropora corals, you'll see dense schools of onespot snappers (Lutjanus monostigma), schools of pennantfish (Heniochus intermedius) hovering immobile as they rock with the moving water, yellowtail surgeonfish (Zebrasoma xanthurum) and pufferfish (Arothron diadematosus), which are especially common near the south tower in the water below the boat mooring area.

Descending along the eastern side, where the drop-off begins at 25 meters deep, you'll be able to spot schools of pelagic fish, especially yellowspotted trevallies (Carangoides fulvoguttatus), tunas and twinspot snapper (Lutjanus bohar), which swim out of the blue depths toward the walls of this reef so rich in potential prey. At the end of the dive, when you've reached the top of the reef, you'll enjoy the fascinating spectacle offered by a myriad of small anthias whose bright orange color paints the surface of the sea.

You can dive any time of the day at Hal Hal, as there will always be a few sides that are perfectly illuminated by the sun. Current permitting, they can be explored fairly easily, in a single descent along the sides of both towers. Anyone lucky enough to discover the waters of Hal Hal will immediately realize that this place is still pristine.

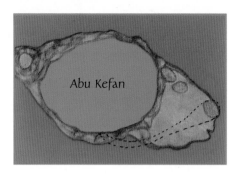

Abu Kefan

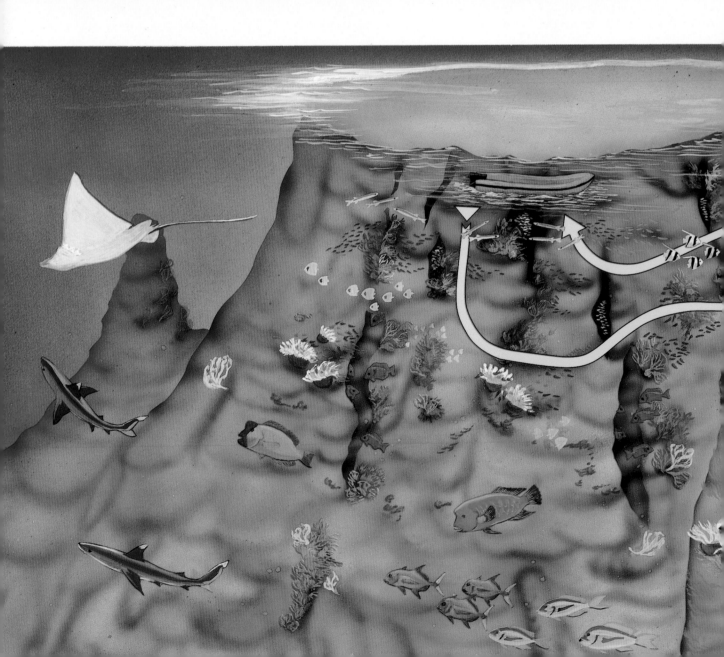

A – Divers may see the elegant shortnoese blacktail shark (Carcharhinus wheeleri) *in the open sea, where the coral walls plunge toward the abyss.*

B – During the day, lionfish (Pterois volitans) *remain hidden in the dense tangle of gorgonians.*

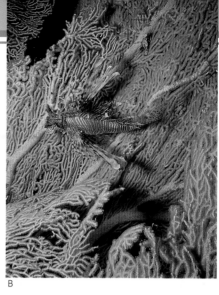

B

Abu Kefan

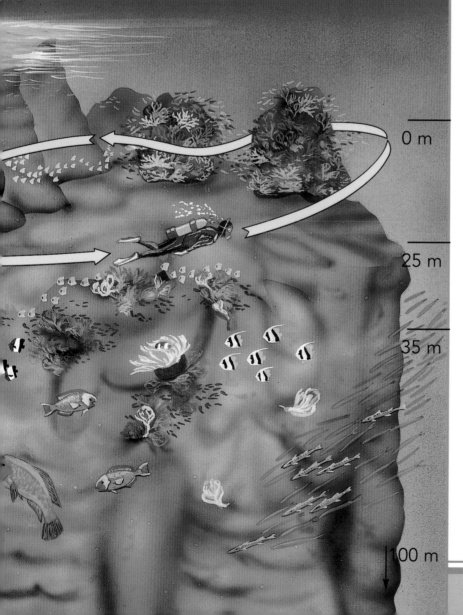

0 m

25 m

35 m

100 m

THE REEF OF ABU KEFAN, which in Arabic means "the deepest zone" is located about a two hour sail southeast of the town of Safaga, and has an elongated form running northwest-southeast. Due to its isolated position in the open sea, the coral reef does not offer a good mooring point for boats, as the north and south sides rise up from depths of over 100 meters and are often swept by waves and currents. For this reason, the anchoring buoys are located at the southwest point, sheltered by a coral formation not far from the reef, which constitutes the only moderately protected zone.

Before beginning your dive, you should carefully evaluate the intensity of the current from the north, which may be quite powerful in these waters.

The most interesting itinerary is the route that runs along the east wall until it comes to the vast plateau, which juts out like a panoramic terrace on the north point.

Once you're in the water, sea conditions permitting, follow the east wall of the reef to a depth of 30-35 meters, where you'll see a constant

A – The walls of this reef are home to splendid branches of gorgonians in a wide variety of sizes and species. Their size is due to the position of the reef, which is always swept by light currents that create ideal conditions for their growth.

B – In the shallower, more illuminated areas of the coral reef, there are extraordinary accumulations of stony corals that create an ideal refuge for a myriad of marine organisms.

A

C

B

succession of majestic sea fans (*Subergorgia hicksoni*) and soft corals, which cover the whole reef with color. The reef has an irregular structure in this area, full of crevices, cracks and small caves, a natural refuge for goggle-eyes (*Priacanthus hamrur*), schools of sweetlips (*Plectorhinchus gaterinus*) and dozens of twobar anemonefish (*Amphiprion bicinctus*) surrounded by their protecting sea anemones.

The main attraction at Abu Kefan is always the large pelagic fish that seem to materialize here as if by magic: silvery schools of barracudas (*Sphyraena barracuda*), bigeye trevallies (*Caranx sexfasciatus*), tunas and reef sharks wander undisturbed in the blue depths. Continuing your dive north, ascend slightly toward the surface until you

reach a depth of 25 meters, where you'll find a vast terrace dotted with coral formations and imposing towers. Numerous sedentary fish like the blotcheye soldierfish (*Myripristis murdjan*), wrasses (*Cheilinus fasciatus*), members of the Labridae family, and turtles swim in this splendid aquarium, heedless of the presence of divers.

One area you shouldn't miss, sea conditions permitting, is the outside edge of the plateau, where the reef forms a wall that plunges vertically, making an excellent observation point for large fish swimming off in the blue depths. You may encounter schools of trevallies, spotted eagle rays (*Aetobatus narinari*) and barracudas, while during the summer you'll frequently encounter magnificent specimens of solitary hammerhead sharks (*Sphyrna lewini*). After carefully exploring this area, come back up to the reef wall that, from a depth of 20 meters to the surface, has a coral environment full of coral fish such as anthias, parrotfish, and butterflyfish (*Chaetodon fasciatus, semilarvatus*) that fill the whole sea floor with color and life.

As you continue south, you'll once again come to the east side of the reef. In this area, you should stay close to the surface because, in just a few meters of water, you can admire the slender silhouettes of needlefish and trumpetfish darting about in search of food. End your dive halfway along the wall, where you'll find the support raft waiting for you. Abu Kefan is probably the most difficult dive in this area, but for this very reason, once you're out of the water, you'll feel exhilarated by your truly extraordinary experiences and sensations.

C – A large tuft of red alcyonarians surrounded by the teeming life of the reef, is another splendid example of the extraordinary biological wealth of the Red Sea.

D – Lunertail groupers (*Variola louti*) live in small groups among the reef corals. The male is usually easily recognizable by his larger size and gaudier colors.

E – It's common to see pelagic fish passing by on the side of the reef more exposed to the currents. This school of barracudas has formed such a dense group that it looks like a marvelous silvery wall.

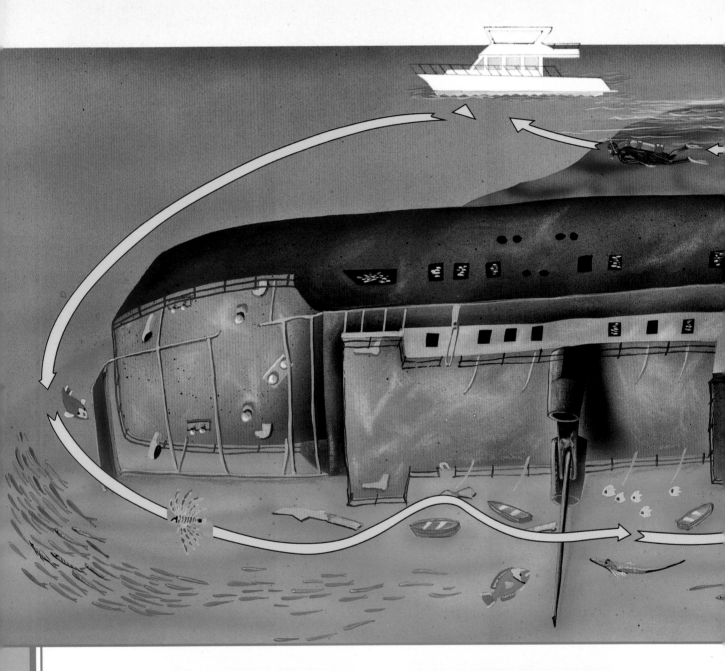

Port Safaga

Panorama Reef

N

Hal Hal

Abu Kefan

Sha'ab Sheer

SALEM EXPRESS

Wreck of Salem Express

ON THE NIGHT OF DECEMBER 15, 1991, the *Salem Express* ferry, which had set sail from the port of Jeddah in Saudi Arabia and was headed for Port Safaga, ended its voyage a little less than 16 kilometers from its port of destination. Due to an unforgivable error by its captain, the ship crashed into a small coral tower not far from the Sha'ab Sheer coral reef.

The ferry hit the reef with such force that it caused the prow hatch to open and water to enter, sinking the ship immediately.

Despite its over 1000 tons of tonnage, the *Salem Express* sank quickly, leaving very little time for the numerous pilgrims returning from Mecca to save themselves. Of the almost one thousand passengers on the ship, over 600 lost their lives in this tragic shipwreck.

The hull now lies perfectly intact near the reef that caused it to founder, with the starboard side resting 32 meters deep and the port side located about 10 meters from the surface. It is easy to reach if you descend along the mooring line attached to a buoy and tied directly to the wreck.

Your exploration of the *Salem Express* will begin from the stern, where you'll find two large propellers

10 m

27 m

32 m

A - The wreck of the Salem Express is recent, so the enormous wooden deck is still completely intact.

B - The rescue boats, the only possibility for survival at the time of the wreck, lie unused on the sea floor.

A

B

A - The characteristic massive, square form of the stern area lies majestically at a depth of 30 meters.

B - Near the aft deck is a metallic structure that covered the quarter-deck. The bollards with cables and an enormous capstan can be distinguished in this part of the ship.

with four blades. The port side propeller stands out impressively, facing upward and surrounded by multitudes of colorful alcyonarians, while the starboard propeller is partially submerged in the sand. Following the imposing wooden bridge on the port side, about halfway up the hull you can see the rescue boats resting on the sea floor 27 meters deep, testimony to how fast the ship went down, not even giving passengers time to use them.

Scattered all around the sea floor are the personal belongings of the passengers.

Proceeding along the bridge, you'll come to two large smokestacks rising majestically into the blue depths. They bear a large letter "S" encircled by a laurel wreath, the initial of the ship's name.

When you reach the ferry's upper deck, near the quarter-deck, the outside radar is clearly visible, and with the aid of a flashlight, the ship's instruments can still be seen on the bridge. You can also explore the innumerable windows, where you'll see completely empty spaces illuminated by the weak rays of light filtering through.

At the prow, you will immediately note the immense hatch that opened in the impact against the reef. Inside, an impressive cloud of glassfish reflect transparently in the beam of your flashlight, while on the left bulwark you can see an enormous anchor attached to the hawsehole.

Diving on this wreck is quite evocative, especially in the morning, when the sun uniformly illuminates the entire hull.

You should not enter the ship, as it is considered a tomb and thus

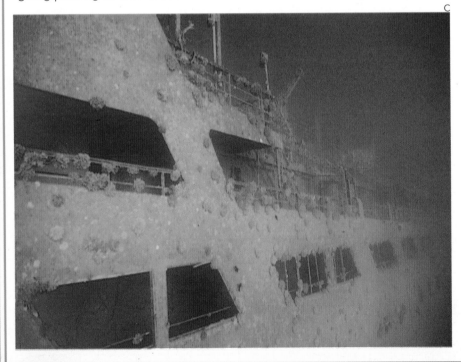

deserves full respect for the numerous victims of this tragic shipwreck. In this area of the reef, the water is usually quite murky, and it is almost always swept by a light current. A dive on the *Salem Express* can be considered somewhat difficult, so move with extreme caution, and always use a buddy system. Although only a decade has passed since the day of the wreck, the hull is already covered with life and colors due to the various species of corals that proliferate abundantly on its wreckage. In addition, schools of small barracudas and trevallies, frequent visitors of the waters around the wreck, have now become a common sight. Going along the stern side, you'll find the buoy mooring line, which you can follow up to your boat.

E

C - A view of the starboard side shows that despite the fact that the Salem Express sank only a short time ago, the coral has already begun its work of colonizing the iron structures.

D - In its impact with the reef, the immense hatch in the bow of the Salem Express fell open, quickly taking in large quantities of water

and causing the ship to sink rapidly. An immense colony of glassfish has colonized the area.

E - The enormous four-bladed propeller to port is raised from the sea floor, while the propeller on the starboard side is semi-submerged. This position away from the light has encouraged the development of large alcyonarians.

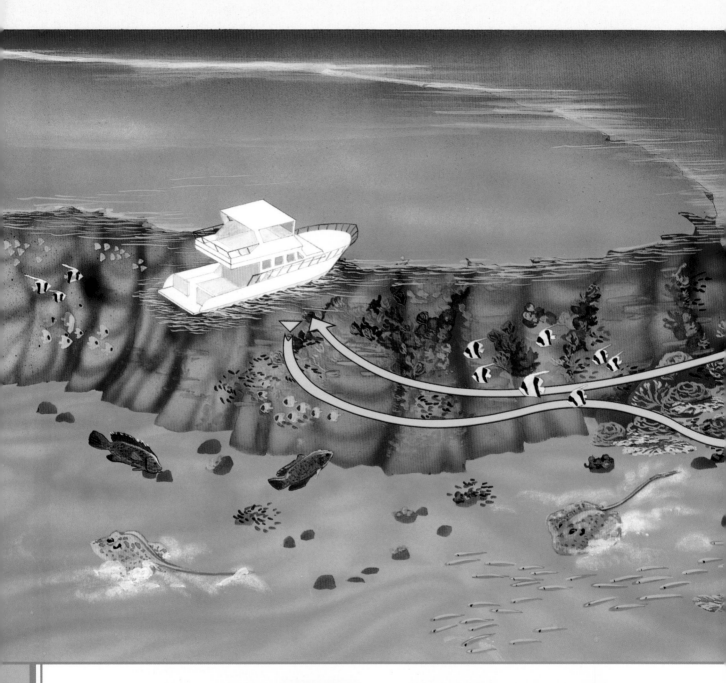

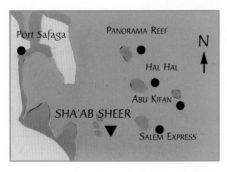

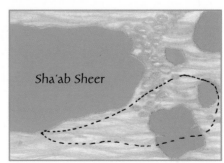

Sha'ab Sheer

Sha'ab Sheer

THE REEF OF SHA'AB SHEER, about an hour and a half sail from the coast of Safaga, consists of a long coral reef in an unmistakable horseshoe form that winds from east to west. It's also easily recognizable by the automatic lighthouse on the western end of the reef. The reef extends for almost a mile toward the open sea, providing diving center boats with safe mooring places in well-sheltered areas located at the far sides of the reef.

The broad coral reef at Sha'ab Sheer offers two distinct diving itineraries. Following the north wall, you can either head to the west tip, go around it and enter the lagoon, where you will find the mooring buoys, or follow the north wall toward the east tip.

The most interesting dive is the one that ends on the east end, where, without exceeding a depth of 15 meters, you'll find one of the most spectacular coral reefs in the whole area, full of coral formations that reach out to the open sea, creating a sort of lunar landscape with an amazing diversity of forms and colors.

Depending on sea conditions and after carefully checking the current, you can dive directly onto the north wall, following it on the right side.

0 m

15 m

20 m

A – With its unique horseshoe shape, the long reef of Sha'ab Sheer offers boats excellent shelter from the strong north winds. The outer wall drops into the blue abyss, while the inner lagoon is less difficult.

A

along the entire side of the reef, where various species of multicolor coral fish swim about. At the perimeter of the towers, you'll see large spotted groupers (*Plectropomus pessuliferus*), morays (*Gymnothorax javanicus*), schools of striped snappers (*Lutjanus kasmira*), and bluestriped snappers (*Lutjanus bohar*) that swim along the reef in a continuous search for prey. In the sandy areas adjacent to the corals, you're likely to encounter large turtles (*Chelonia mydas*), which during the summer months come to the reef at Sha'ab Sheer. When you reach the outer area of the plateau, where the floor slopes down out to the open sea, re-enter near the main reef, keeping the wall on the right. Here you'll find an impressive

A – One of the most interesting characteristics of sea turtles is their sense of direction. Once females have reached sexual maturity, they always return to the beach where they were born to deposit their eggs.

Along this route following the current, you'll see a wall full of cracks, where small gorgonians have grown alternately with colorful alcyonarians. Following the base of the wall, you'll find various coral conformations that hide the big little secrets of the sea. When you reach the east tip, you'll find an impressive maze of *Pachyseris rugosa* stony coral formations, commonly known as brain corals, connected to other massive coral formations that are the most interesting aspect of this dive. The central tower, by far the most beautiful, is totally surrounded by a myriad of soft corals growing

E

F

canyon of Acropora and Porites. During the exploration of this section of the floor, be very cautious when you move about to admire every detail of this natural spectacle, and avoid inadvertently striking the extremely fragile stony corals. If the current or sea conditions outside the reef are not favorable for diving as we have described, you can enter the water directly from the boat mooring area and from here go to the east point, where you can explore the coral towers located on the outside. After going around them, you can then return to your starting point.

The best time to dive is mid-morning, when the sun completely illuminates the floor. At about 15-20 meters deep, it will be a pleasant excursion through a fantastic coral garden.

B – During the day, sabre squirrelfish (Sargocentron spiniferum) remain motionless within caves or under the vaults of large corals, while at night they leave their hiding places and move to the more open areas of the reef.

C – Little scalefin anthias (Pseudanthias squamipinnis) females have orange scales with a wide pink band on their flanks, while males are a more pronounced red, with a deeply incised, falcate tail.

D – The Epibulus insidiator wrasse is a shy creature whose ideal habitat is reefs with a wealth of intricate coral formations, where it can easily hide. It has well-developed lips with prominent teeth similar to fangs.

E – The bluestriped snapper (Lutjanus kasmira) is one of the most graceful fish in the Red Sea. It has a tapered body and bright yellow flanks, with four gray-edged light blue longitudinal stripes.

F – The blotcheye soldierfish (Myripristis murdjan) has gaudy silvery-red scales and large black eyes. It usually lives in schools and is nocturnal in habits.

El Quseir

THE TOWN OF EL QUSEIR, located 80 km south of Safaga and 140 kilometers from Hurghada, has become one of the new tourist centers to spring up along the southern coast of the Egyptian Red Sea.

The ambitious project to restore the old city, which began in 1998 by a Swedish organization on behalf of UNESCO, includes plans for reconstructing the urban fabric and five hundred dwellings; it will soon turn the little town into one of the most attractive tourist areas on the coast.

El Quseir is the only existing example of the ancient architecture typical of the Egyptian Red Sea, and was built with the only material easily available in this area: coral rock. The construction technique, unchanged over the centuries, is absolutely the most suitable for weather conditions in this area: walls are well insulated from the heat, with openings positioned in a way that carries the ocean breeze into the homes. All buildings have wide balconies of carved wood, known as "Masharabiye," which allowed Arab women to look out without being seen by passers-by.

The origins of El Quseir date back to the Ptolmaic period, when the port of Leukos Limen developed, a commercial port of vital strategic importance for ships that plied the waters of the Red Sea. The city was located at the beginning of the main route that connected the coast with the Nile Valley. Consequently, despite the birth of new commercial ports like that of Berenice located 200 kilometers to the south, Leukos Limen continued to play a major role in trade that continued even during the Greco-Roman epoch.

In the early 16th century, during the period of great geographical discoveries, numerous navigators crossed this sea. The Portuguese were the first to follow these routes, which then became trading routes between the ancient Mediterranean world and the new East Indies. At that time, the port of El Quseir, like Suakin in Sudan, was an obligatory crossroads for traders.

In the following centuries, the town continued to develop its commercial power until, in the 19th century, the port of El Quseir became the primary port of embarkation for pilgrims on their way to Mecca.

Today there is tangible evidence of this glorious past in the old dwellings in the historic center and fortress, built in the 16th century by Sultan Selim to defend the port.

The mountains behind the city are rich in minerals and phosphates. To make the best use of these natural resources, in the early 1900s an Italian mining company built an immense mining facility that was in operation until just a few years ago, providing employment for many inhabitants. The plant, now closed, is part of a recovery plan in an industrial archaeology project.

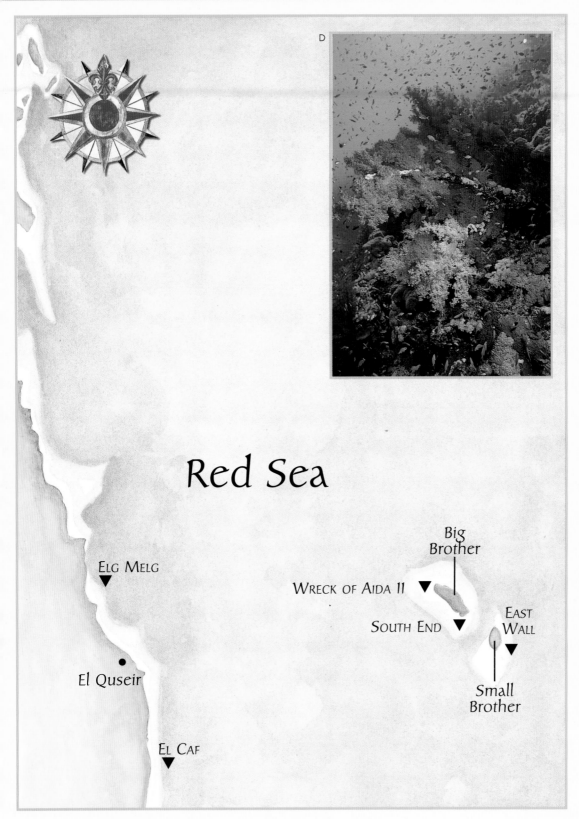

Red Sea

ELG MELG ▼

El Quseir ●

EL CAF ▼

WRECK OF AIDA II ▼

Big Brother

SOUTH END ▼

EAST WALL ▼

Small Brother

A – This portal marks the entrance to the fortress that Sultan Selim built in the 16th century to defend the port. The entire fortress was recently rebuilt and reopened to the public, through the efforts of a group of Swedish archaeologists.

B – Big Brother Island is distinguished by the lighthouse built by the English in the late 19th century. On the southwest side is a wooden pier that provides access to the island.

C - The fishing fleet is still active in the Quseir area, and fisherman stand at the water's edge, intent on repairing the nets that will soon be lowered into the water for yet another catch of fish.
In recent years, the number of fishermen has greatly decreased, and many of them have embarked on less strenuous and probably more profitable activities.

D – Clusters of pink alcyonarians cover the marvelous walls of Brothers' Islands, while a myriad of small anthias drifts with the current.

Most of the diving areas accessible from El Quseir are along the long coastal reef. This area is full of splendid underwater seascapes with unusual inhabitants like the sea cow, which has become extremely rare due to the senseless hunting that went on for many years in the Red Sea.

As present, the coastal area is scattered with hotels, built a few kilometers north of the old port city. Among these, the prestigious Movenpick Jolie Village stands out. It was built in classical Nubian style with cupolas in pink sandstone, overlooking an enchanting "Bay of Sirens," with a coral reef a few meters from the beach. One of the most interesting diving areas is located 53 kilometers east of the coast of El Quseir, where you'll find the solitary Brothers' Islands, whose Arabic name is "El Akhawein," or "brothers" They are two small islands rising like two columns in the middle of the Red Sea, from an abyss over 300 meters deep. Due to their special position, these islands boast one of the most fascinating, pristine environments of the whole Red Sea.

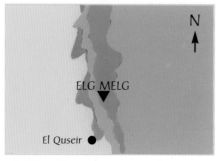

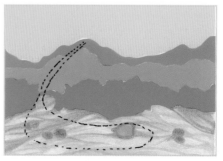

ELG MELG

El Quseir ●

N

Elg Melg

T HE ELG MELG AREA is located 30 kilometers north of El Quseir, so the diving area can be reached by taking the coastal road in the diving center's jeep. Once you reach the exact spot, located in the lee of the coast, enter the water directly from the beach and drop into a long underwater canyon that cuts the reef at right angles. Right from the start, this spectacular passage shows a large variety of stony corals covered with alcyonarians and small gorgonians, around which swim a myriad of small, multicolored coral fish, such as yellowfin goatfish (*Mulloides vanicolensis*), Indo-pacific sergeant majors (*Abudefduf vaigiensis*), wrasses, and compact schools of masked butterflyfish (*Chaethodon semilarvatus*).

Proceeding toward the base of the reef, you reach a depth of 35 meters, where corals in a wide variety of shapes extend over a vast sandy plateau from which several isolated stony coral structures rise. Observing carefully, and with a bit of luck, you

25 m

35 m

A

A – Small sergeant majors (Abudefduf vaigiensis), with their graceful black and white stripes, live in dense schools not far from the shallower areas of the reef, where they often create splendid carousels around divers.

A – The fire coral (Millepora dichotoma) *has a tree-like, yellowish brown appearance with white-tipped branches. The polyps that form the skeleton of these hydrozoans are extremely stinging, and when touched will cause a painful burning sensation.*

B – *Sea turtles reproduce in the spring and summer, when they dig nests up to 50 cm deep on the more isolated beaches, where the females deposit about a hundred eggs in each nest. The eggs hatch in about two months.*

known as fire coral, which, if touched, will produce severe rashes similar to burns. At the edge of this small reef, where the corals end in the sand, it's common to see large turtles (*Eretmochelys imbricata*) which you may be able to approach if you're cautious. By carefully examining the area at the edge of the tower, you can easily spot thin pipefish (*Corythoichthys schultzi*) moving vertically among the cracks in the rocks, in search of the small crustaceans on which they feed.

When you've finished exploring the reef, return to the coastal wall and rise to a shallower depth. Keeping the wall to your right, return to the canyon where you began your dive. Along this entire stretch of reef you can admire the spectacle of hundreds of anthias and surgeonfish filling the top of the reef with color.

A dive on Elg Melg is rather simple, and you should stay within a depth of 30 meters. At this depth, you can easily observe the various environments of this reef, whose beauty and brilliant colors make it look like an immense aquarium. The best time to dive is the morning or early afternoon, when the sunlight uniformly illuminates the floor, even further enhancing its colors.

may spot the form of a beautiful sedentary leopard shark (*Triakis semifasciata*) resting on the sandy floor, as well as numerous bluespotted lagoon rays (*Taeniura lymna*), torpedoes (*Torpedo sinuspersici*) and small gobies like *Ctenogobius maculosus*, which share their den dug in the sand with a tiny, almost invisible shrimp from the Alpheidae family.

Once again approaching the coral wall, proceed north, keeping the reef to your left. Here you may spot gray morays (*Siderea grisea*) hidden

among the corals, large peacock groupers (*Cephalopolis argus*) and schools of onespot snappers (*Lutjanus monostigma*), while, gazing out to the open sea, you may encounter schools of silvery *Platax*.

After traveling a brief stretch at 25 meters deep, you'll come to a large coral tower slightly separated from the main reef, which rises majestically from the sand. All around this tower are numerous stony corals, including large Acropora umbrellas and the delicate lacework structures of *Millepora dichotoma*, commonly

D

C – The whitebelly damselfish (Amblyglyphidodon leucogaster), which measures up to about 10 cm in length, lives in small groups near corals, where it takes immediate refuge as soon as it senses any danger.

D – The round form of the bluespotted lagoon stingray (Taeniura lymna), which can reach as much as two meters in length, is a common sight in sandy areas sheltered by large Acropora corals.

E – Due to their extraordinarily flat, streamlined form, batfish (Platax orbicularis) are able to remain perfectly motionless in the blue depths of the open sea, even when the reef is swept by powerful cu rrents.

E

El Caf

IT'S NOT EASY to give an exact description of a dive at El Caf, as an exploration of this area includes a fantastic maze of countless coral structures rising from a bed of white sand. The diving area is located about 10 kilometers south of El Quseir, taking the coastal road by jeep, and then proceeding on another few hundred meters to the precise entry point, which lies in the shelter of a lagoon.

Your descent begins by jumping in directly from the shore, near a broad canyon that cuts the reef in a perpendicular line. It is wide enough to allow divers to pass through, but be very careful of your position to avoid destroying the delicate coral structures.

When you reach the end of the canyon, follow the wall on the right after crossing a short sandy stretch. Here you may see skillfully camouflaged bluespotted lagoon

24 m

A

rays (*Taeniura lymna*) and crocodilefish (*cociella crocodila*) on the sandy seabed. You will then come to a solitary coral tower rising out of the seabed. Begin your exploration of this large pinnacle and the countless corals all around it, with its intricate structure concealing schools of goggle-eyes (*Priacanthus hamrur*), motionless under the broad Acropora fans.

A – Two examples of the nudibranch (Chromodoris quadricolor) are feeding on the surface layer of a red sponge. These mollusks can be seen on coral seabeds only a few meters deep, down to a depth of 30 meters.

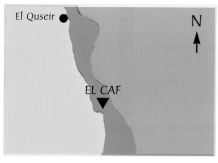

El Quseir

N

EL CAF

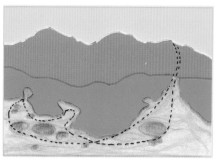

A – Using its strong beak, the titan triggerfish (Balistoides viridescens) digs a large circular nest in the coral sea bed, where it will fiercely defend its eggs from any invaders who enter its territory.

B – The warty slug (Phyllidia varicosa) has a perfect defense system. If a fish tries to attack it, it emits an extremely pungent, poisonous toxin that quickly repels any aggressor.

C – The little hawkfish (Paracirrhites forsteri) likes to lie in wait among the larger branches of coral, from which it can quickly launch successful attacks against its prey.

At the base of the tower, you'll find various crevices and small cracks framed by yellow gorgonians, while schools of glassfish (Parapriacanthus guentheri) move within the most hidden recesses, creating magical sights with their constant movements. Observing carefully, you may spot tiny shrimp, colorful nudibranchs, and an infinite number of small inhabitants of the sea, usually overlooked because of their small size, but still absolutely fundamental in maintaining the fragile balance of underwater life. When you've completed your exploration of this coral tower, once again move to the lee of the main wall, to discover the more southerly areas of El Caf. Following the profile of the reef on the right side, you'll see an extraordinary variety of stony coral structures which have welded together to dauntlessly resist the

D – The red branches of this sponge are a favorite food of many species of nudibranchs, which manage to cover their outer tissues with the calcareous spicules they take from the sponges, fashioning a sort of armor.

E – A pair of Red Sea bannerfish (Heniochus intermedius) with their unmistakable striped color, surveys a large Goniopora stony coral formation, with fully expanded polyps.

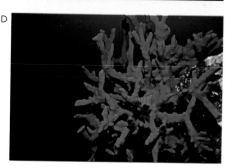

destructive force of the waves.

A sheltered inlet contains the most interesting area of the entire dive: a series of pinnacles rising vertically from a sandy plateau at a depth of 24 meters, reaching heights of about a dozen meters, with the walls totally covered with soft corals and alcyonarians, forming splendid patterns of light and color. Each individual tower seems perfectly detailed, with a succession of arches

and caves in which schools of cardinal fish (Apogon aureus), large spotted groupers (Plectropomus pessuliferus), and poisonous scorpionfish like Scorpaenopsis oxycephala find refuge. Ascending to the top of the towers, you can easily spot small trevallies and dentex intent on pursuing hapless coral fish. At the base of the massive structures are wide sandy areas, which at first look uninteresting but which should

actually be explored with some care, as the sandy sediment conceals spotted rays, crocodilefish and various types of gobies (Valenciennea puellaris, sexguttata, Amblyeleotris steinitzi).

After admiring the spectacle of this magical coral environment, it's time to return. Using the left wall of the reef as a reference, follow it until you reach the canyon, where your dive ends and you re-surface.

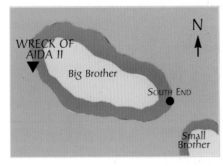

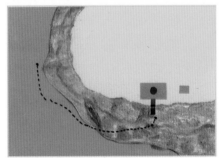

WRECK OF
AIDA II

Big Brother

SOUTH END

Small
Brother

N

Wreck
of
Aida II

O N THE NIGHT OF SEPTEMBER 16, 1957, the *Aida II*, an Egyptian ship carrying military personnel responsible for checking lighthouses, was attempting to dock on the west side of Big Brother. The wind was blowing violently, and the great waves that battered the coast struck the ship with such force that they slammed it against the northwestern wall of the island. Then, repeatedly crashing against the sharp reef caused the hull to break into two pieces, and the ship began to leak large quantities of water, causing it to sink. Thanks to quick rescue efforts by the ship *Bergheus*, which had received the S.O.S. from the *Aida II*, the shipwreck fortunately resulted in no fatalities for the 140 Egyptian soldiers aboard.

More than 40 years have now passed since the accident, and the *Aida II*, peacefully resting on the wall of the reef, still upright with its bow at a depth of 27 meters and the stern at 68 meters, is one of the most fascinating shipwrecks in the Red Sea.

As this is an area subject to strong winds, the diving area, located at the north point of the island, is reached with the aid of a raft, while the boat will stay moored in the southern area.

Dive in and quickly reach a depth of 25 meters, keeping the wall to your left. From this point, the strong current will lead you directly perpendicular to the ship.

0 m

27 m

40 m

68 m

A – The stern of the Aida, which sank off the largest of the Brothers' Islands, lies over 60 meters deep. Sunk in 1957, the ship rests in a vertical position off the northwest coast of the island.

A

A

B

C An excellent reference to pinpoint the location of the hull of the *Aida II* is several encrusted windlasses and bollards over the corals, which were probably thrown off the ship when it struck the reef. Right below them is the imposing profile of the hull, and from here you can begin to explore this truly spectacular wreck. The first sight of it will leave you breathless, as the ship looks like a flowering garden, completely enveloped by multicolor alcyonarians, swollen and rich with oxygen due to the constant presence of currents in these waters. Your exploration will begin from the upper deck located about 40 meters deep, where several hatchways are visible that permit access to the hold, now completely empty of cargo and an ideal refuge for thousands of little glassfish. The sunlight, which barely

penetrates these areas, is quite dim, and you'll need a flashlight to illuminate the inner areas of the ship. Be very careful of the sharp wreckage of the hull. After examining the hold, note how each outer section of the hull is completely covered with countless colorful organisms: splendid alcyonarians, gorgonians, anemones, and sponges.

All around you is an explosion of life and movement: clouds of anthias circle through the wreckage, groups of Indian lionfish, morays

A – Pictured here is a detail of the Aida's aft guardrail, enveloped by multicolored alcyonarians.

B – A small sea anemone, shown here with its clownfish, has settled on the metallic structures of the shipwreck, surrounded by colorful formations of soft corals.

C – A massive conformation of (Heteroxenia fuscescens) has grown along the structures of the wreck, following its form.

(*Gymnothorax javanicus*) and small groupers peep out of air inlets and other safe hiding places, while trevallies, barracudas, and sharks are common in the open water. With a bit of luck, you may even see a solitary ray (*Aetobatus narinari*). When you finish your dive on the *Aida II*, ascend back up along the ridge and continue at a shallower depth following the wall to the south. Carried by the current, you can admire this luxuriant, lush coral life. Every area is equally beautiful, and everywhere you'll see an explosion of colors and forms. Time will pass quickly, and the little air still left will allow you to reach the landing area on the island. From here, using the rafts that have followed the divers from the surface the entire time, you can return to the moored boat.

D – Great numbers of anthias are present everywhere in the upper zones of the wreck, giving life to this ship resting silently along the wall of the reef.

E – The entire wreck is surrounded by enormous formations of soft corals which, due to the constant current, are rich in oxygen and quite turgid.

F – This is what remains of the bow section of the Aida, resting on the coral walls 27 meters deep.

A

B

A – From the lighthouse you can see the mooring area used by cruise boats on the south point facing the stretch of sea separating the larger island from Small Brother.

B – The Brothers' Islands are located in the middle of the Red Sea, between the Egyptian coast of El Quseir and the coast of Saudi Arabia.

Big Brother (South End)

0 m

40 m

THE LARGEST OF THE BROTHERS' ISLANDS is flat and uniform, 400 meters long and a little less than 40 meters wide, and has a splendid lighthouse on the west side.

After the Suez Canal was opened on September 11, 1869, an increasing number of ships began to cross this perilous stretch of sea, especially English ships headed to the colonies in India. In order to provide better assistance to the convoys, beginning in 1880, the British Empire established a series of outposts in order to guarantee maximum navigation safety. One of these was the old and glorious Big Brother lighthouse, built by Chance Bros. of Birmingham. It was an oil lamp whose weak light was strengthened by an efficient system of Fresnel lenses, making the light visible up to a distance of 27 kilometers.

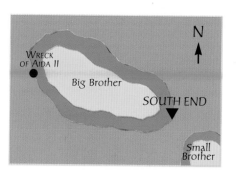

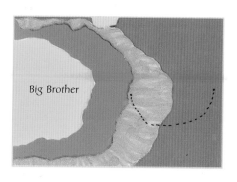

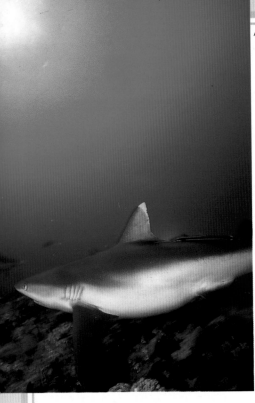

A – The shortnose blacktail shark (Carcharinus wheeleri) is quite common along the coral walls of the Brothers' Islands, as these islands rising vertically from the abyss are an ideal habitat for large pelagic fish.

B – Pelagic fish tend to congregate where the current is most powerful, and it's not uncommon to see schools of bigeye trevallies (Caranx sexfasciatus) forming an impenetrable wall glittering with silvery reflections.

The rotation of the complex optical system, which weighed over a ton, depended on a perfect internal mechanism of cords and counterweights that rose and fell the entire length of the lighthouse. This fascinating system of counterweights functioned perfectly until 1994, when it was replaced by a more modern, efficient system. It lost its charm, but guaranteed greater safety to the numerous ships that cross this stretch of sea every year.

Dives on the south end begin directly from the boat, moored to the only buoy on the island. Follow the line to the lee of the wall, and from here begin your dive. Due to the extraordinary transparency of the water, as you gradually descend into the blue depths, you'll feel the marvelous sensation of being suspended in the void, until you reach a broad plateau that projects outward. Here you'll find an incessant succession of walls alternating with small stony coral plateaus, the undisputed reign of sharks, barracudas and tunas.

In the center of the first plateau, 40 meters deep, is a large stony coral formation, a shelter for splendid coral fish. But the most spectacular element is a solitary gorgonian fan that opens majestically like a gigantic hand.

Magnificent specimens of silver-tipped gray sharks wander the open sea, totally indifferent to human presence, while schools of trevallies and barracudas hover in the water, allowing themselves to be transported by the current. The walls bordering the plateau fall vertically into the abyss, and hammerhead sharks swim out from the blue depths, often approaching curiously from above the plateau, to vanish once again into the depths.

If visibility and currents permit it, it's worthwhile to go out toward the outer wall of the point, always using the broad terrace as a landmark, to watch pelagic fish swimming off in the deep blue sea. Continue your dive at shallower depths, and following the current, briefly go along the wall, which will be completely covered with alcyonarians and splendid stony coral formations. Gazing out to the open sea, you'll immediately note the enormous variety of pelagic fish present in these waters, primarily

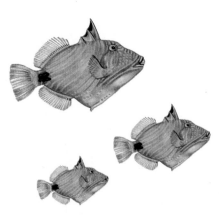

schools of tunas and trevallies swimming undisturbed near the surface. With a bit of luck, you may even spot a magnificent solitary hammerhead shark, the true lord of this part of the sea.

The best time to dive on the south end of Big Brother is mid-morning, when the sunlight perfectly illuminates the sea floor, setting off the fantastic colors of the reef.

C – A little before sunset, a school of small fish darts quickly below the surface of the sea, the warm sunlight glinting off their shiny scales.

D – When diving in these solitary areas of the Red Sea, it's important to stop your exploration of the reef from time to time and look out to the open sea, where it's easy to spot large sharks or splendid trevallies passing by.

E – An underwater encounter with a large shark is no cause for alarm, as these animals are generally quite shy and peaceful. In fact, you may find it rather difficult to get close enough to them to take a good photograph.

F – Divers in the waters off Brothers' Islands may also have a magnificent encounter with barracudas, which form silvery schools of sometimes hundreds of individuals.

E

A

A – The only beach on the coast of the two islands is the stretch of fine coral sand on the south side of Small Brother. During the summer, hundreds of swallows gather at the base of the island to lay their eggs.

Small Brother (East Wall)

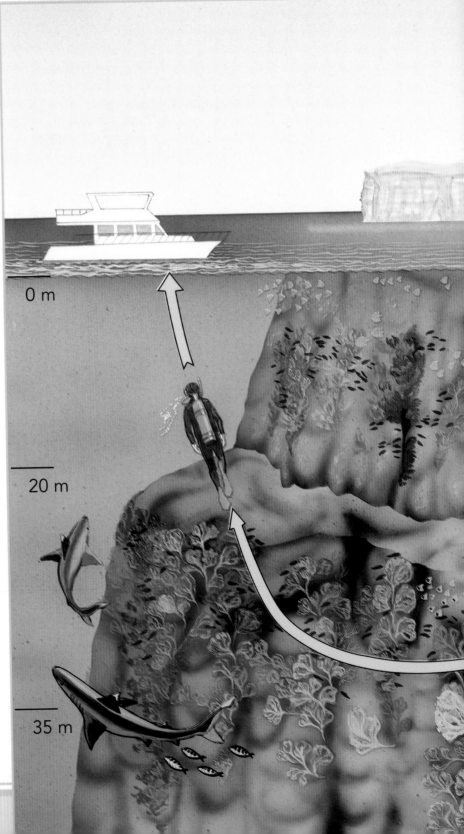

0 m

20 m

35 m

THE SMALLER OF THE BROTHERS' ISLANDS is located 1,6 kilometers away from its larger sibling and is flat and circular in form. When you approach the island by boat, you'll immediately notice the deafening noise of hundreds of terns and sea swallows, who rise in flight to create a magical atmosphere. The extraordinary position of the Brothers' Islands, between the Egyptian and Arabian coasts, has allowed these waters to preserve a precious, uncontaminated oasis of underwater life, as they are the only islands in a part of the sea stretching a hundred miles north and a hundred south.

A dive on the east wall of Small Brother can without doubt be considered one of the best in the world. Indeed, these waters contain

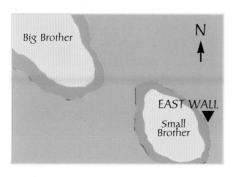

Big Brother

N

EAST WALL

Small Brother

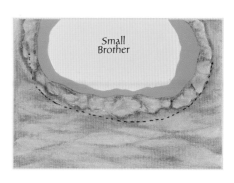

Small Brother

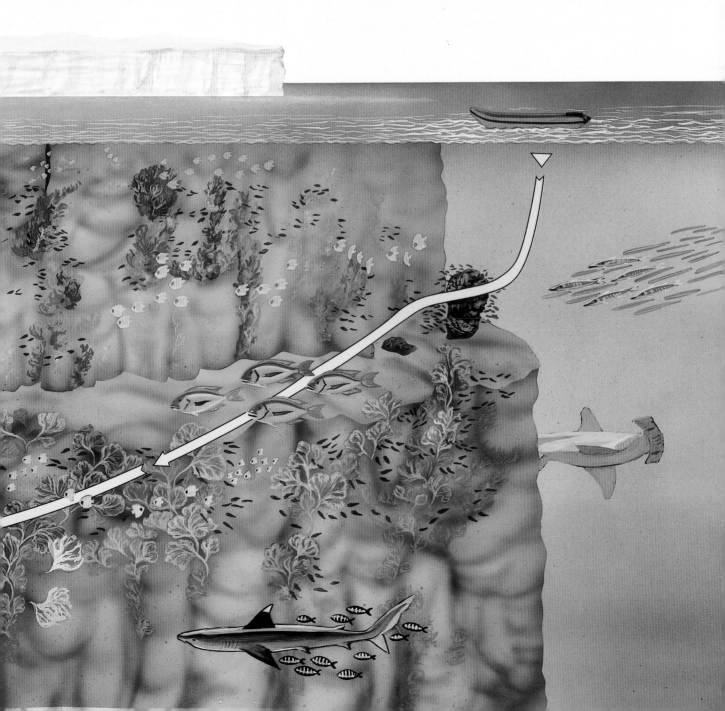

everything this marvelous sea has to offer, due to the ever-present current that creates perfect conditions for this extraordinary marine habitat.

Its walls drop vertically into the abyss, with a constant succession of crevices and corals that vanish into the deep blue, where a wide variety of large predators swims undisturbed in the depths.

Your exploration, which will be a drift dive, begins near the north side of the island, then follows the current along the entire edge of the barrier, keeping the reef to your right, until you come to the sheltered waters of the south coast, where the moored boats wait for divers at the end of their exploration.

As soon as you enter the water, go directly to the wall to avoid being carried out toward the open sea by the current. The raft should always follow the divers' bubbles from the surface in order to assist you during the whole dive. When you reach the coral reef, you'll find a chasm that plunges vertically into the abyss, giving you the extraordinary sensation of being in an absolute void. Although you'll certainly be tempted by the amazing transparency of the water,

A – Anyone diving in the waters off Brothers' Islands will have a chance to see barracudas, whose tapered, streamlined bodies let them swim fearlessly even in the most powerful currents.

B – Extraordinary gorgonian forests grow on the eastern side of the island, making these waters look like an immense enchanted garden.

C – The strong currents that sweep the islands attract numerous barracudas to the coral walls in search of prey. Traveling in schools of hundreds of individuals, they make a spectacular, thrilling sight.

D – Alcyonarians are certainly one of the most showy aspects of the coral reef, and their dense presence creates true underwater gardens in the most magnificent shades of red, violet and lilac.

B

C

A

you won't need to descend to great depths, as even within the first 35 meters you can see all the coral species present, with long branches of black coral, alcyonarians, and a forest of impressively large sea fans (*Subergorgia hicksoni*) that make the east floor of Small Brother one of the most unique places in the Red Sea.

Exploring this wall is truly a fantastic experience. As the current carries you, you'll feel like you're gliding over an infinite stretch of corals and gorgonians, while at your side sharks, bigeye trevallies (*Caranx sexfasciatus*), blackfin barracudas (*Sphyraena qenie*) and magnificent tunas swim undisturbed.

Halfway down the reef, you can admire the remarkable sight of a forest of giant gorgonians, growing vertically from a depth of 35 meters up to just a few meters from the surface, over an area more than two

hundred meters long. There is no other place where you can see such a marvel of nature. Faced with such an extraordinary spectacle, time will pass all too quickly, preventing you from fully enjoying this sight. The gray reef sharks (*Carcharhinus amblyrhynchos*), hammerhead sharks (*Sphyrna lewini*), a splendid solitary *Carcharinus longimanus* and three magnificent moonfish will bring you back to reality.

After the thrill of seeing these magnificent creatures, continue your dive at shallower depths until you reach an area with absolutely no current at all, on the south side of the island not far from the boat mooring area.

You should dive during the early morning hours, when the sunlight illuminates the entire reef, making the colors of the barrier even more vivid.

GINGLYMOSTOMATIDAE FAMILY

Tawny nurse shark
Nebrius ferrugineus

Tapered body, flattened across the belly. The mouth is set forward with respect to the eyes. The snout is marked by two moderately long barbels. The first dorsal fin is larger and taller than the second ones and the anal fin. The coloring is gray-brown, and varies in shade from specimen to specimen according to habitat. This shark is active by night, and by day it tends to remain in the nooks and crannies of the coral reef. It feeds on fish and cephalopods. It measures two to two and a half meters in length.

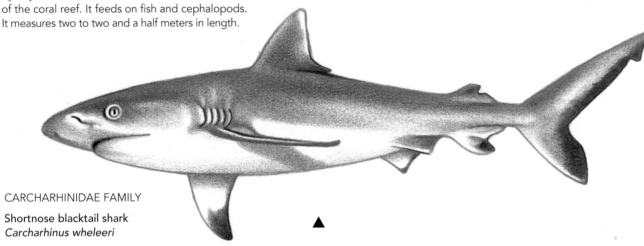

CARCHARHINIDAE FAMILY

Shortnose blacktail shark
Carcharhinus wheleeri

Very similar to the gray reef shark (*Carcharhinus amblyrhynchos*), from which it differs by slightly diverse coloring. The dorsal fin is slightly sickle-shaped and has a whitish, somewhat rounded tip, while the back of the tail fin has a black edge preceded by a bright white stripe. The snout is of moderate length and is distinctly rounded. The eyes are round. It measures one and a half to two meters in length. It is not uncommon at depths between ten and fifty meters.

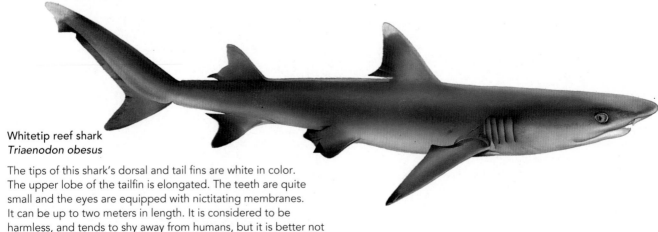

Whitetip reef shark
Triaenodon obesus

The tips of this shark's dorsal and tail fins are white in color. The upper lobe of the tailfin is elongated. The teeth are quite small and the eyes are equipped with nictitating membranes. It can be up to two meters in length. It is considered to be harmless, and tends to shy away from humans, but it is better not to underestimate this shark and to consider it - as many maintain - to be dangerous to humans. It seems to have territorial behavior.

MOBULIDAE FAMILY

Giant manta
Manta birostris

◄ Easily recognized by the well developed pectoral fins that can attain five to six meters in width. The head is projecting from the body, and is distinguished by a pair of long, flat, flexible cephalic fins, separated by the large arch of the mouth.
The upper jaw is devoid of teeth. The spineless tail is long and slim. The dorsal coloring is dark, while the ventral coloring is quite light with dark blotches that can be referred to in order to distinguish one specimen from another.

MYLIOBATIDAE FAMILY

Spotted eagle ray
Aetobatus narinari

This ray can be recognized easily by the pointed and convex head with large eyes and broad lateral spiracles. The body is diamond-shaped and has broad, pointed pectoral fins.
The tail, with one, two, or three denticulated spines, is about three times the length of the body.
The ventral fins are broad and fleshy. The back is dark in coloring, with many small white spots.
The disk-shaped body measures up to two meters in width. It attains a total length of up to two and a half meters. It can also be found in shallow lagoons (one to five meters in depth) on sandy bottoms.

DASYATIDAE FAMILY

Bluespotted lagoon ray
Taeniura lymna

◄ A more or less elongated disk-shaped body, unadorned in the young rays and marked by a series of denticles at the center of the back in the adults. The coloring is grayish brown or yellowish brown on the back, with bluish spots; the belly is light in color. The tail, with one or two poisonous spines at the tip, has bluish stripes along its sides. The disk-shaped body may grow to about one meter in width. At times, the overall length may be greater than two meters. It lives on sandy bottoms at the base of reefs.

SYNODONTIDAE FAMILY

Lizardfish
Synodus variegatus

Elongated body, compressed lengthwise. The head is convex toward the rear base. Eyes in an anterior-dorsal position. The snout is pointed, but short. The mouth is wide, and slightly oblique. The jaws are well developed and equipped with numerous needle-shaped teeth. The coloring is variable, but is generally brownish on the back with more or less distinct red spots on the sides. This fish prefers sandy bottoms where it waits in ambush, poised on its sizable ventral fins. It measures from twenty-fi ve to thirty centimeters.

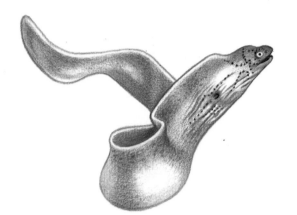

MURAENIDAE FAMILY

Gray moray
Siderea grisea

Small moray with a tapered body and pointed snout, with hard-to-see nares. The mouth is equipped with conical teeth that are more numerous on the upper jaw. The head is brownish, with evident stripes on the back and between the eyes, made up of a series of aligned black points. The rest of the body has a pale brown coloring with violet nuances and brownish marbling. The young are lighter in color. It is not uncommon to see these morays swim in the open on underwater meadowlands. They measure forty to forty-five centimeters in length.

Giant moray
Gymnothorax javanicus

This is the largest of the morays and is fairly common all across the Red Sea. The body is powerful, rather tall on the trunk, and ends in a very well developed head. The snout is short. The mouth is wide. The openings of the opercules are large and black and quite evident. The body is marked by three rows of dark brown spots. The tail is reticulated. It can grow to be as long as two and a half meters.

PLOTOSIDAE FAMILY

Striped eel catfish
Plotosus lineatus

This is a social fish found along coastal reefs and near underwater meadowlands. It is easily recognized by the four barbels that surround its mouth. The second dorsal, the caudal, and the anal fin are connected one to the other. The adults are dark on their backs and have two white longitudinal stripes. The young have bright yellow barbels and fins. The dorsal and pectoral fins have serrated spinous rays connected with poison glands, therefore it is not advisable to handle these fish. They measure from thirty to thirty-five centimeters in length.

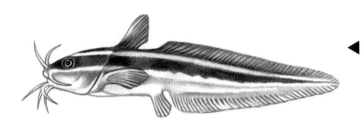

FISTULARIIDAE FAMILY

Cornetfish
Fistularia commersonii

A cylindrical body that ends in a long and tubular snout. The dorsal and anal fins are symmetrical and set quite far back. The two central rays of the caudal fin are very fine and elongated. The coloring is variable, due to the remarkable capacity for camouflage which this fish possesses and uses to capture - from ambush - the small prey on which it feeds. It is common to see this fish swim along, hidden by the body of a larger, but harmless, fish, so as to steal up unnoticed upon its prey. This fish measures up to a meter and a half in length.

ANTENNARIIDAE FAMILY

Frogfish
Antennarius coccineus

A stout and rounded body, rather tall, so that this fish is a fairly clumsy swimmer. The fish of this species move slowly and at times make use of their pectoral and ventral fins to "walk" on the seabed. Particularly distinctive is the transformation of the first ray on the dorsal fin, which is used as bait to attract prey. Coloring is quite variable, but always well camouflaged. It lives among coral reefs, at times using its pectoral fins to clutch the coral branches. It measures fifteen centimeters in length

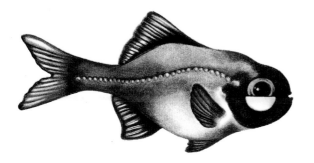

ANOMALOPIDAE FAMILY

Flashlight fish
Photoblepharon palpebratus

Body with an oval shape, a short snout, a truncated forward profile. The eyes are extremely well developed, and beneath them is a large elliptical light-generating organ, which contains luminescent bacteria. This fish is capable of lighting up or extinguishing this organ by raising or lowering a flap of skin. Dark gray in color, this is a typically nocturnal fish. It measures up to twelve centimeters in length.

HOLOCENTRIDAE FAMILY

Blotcheye soldierfish
Myripristis murdjan

Oval body, moderately compressed and high, covered with stinging scales. The first dorsal fin has some ten well developed spinous rays. The eyes are large. The mouth is wide. The coloring is bright red. This is essentially a nocturnal fish, which remains at the entrance to its grotto during the day, as if it were keeping watch. It attains a length of up to thirty centimeters.

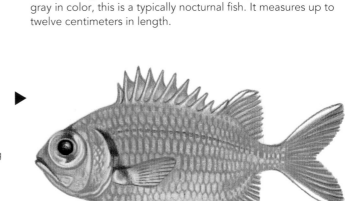

CROWN SQUIRRELFISH
Sargocentron diadema

Oval body, longer and less tall than that of the *Sargocentron spiniferum* species. The eyes are quite large as this too is a species with nocturnal habits. The coloring is red, with evident white stripes on the sides. A white band runs around the lower portion of the face as far as to the opercules. The forward section of the dorsal fin is black. It measures twenty-five centimeters in length.

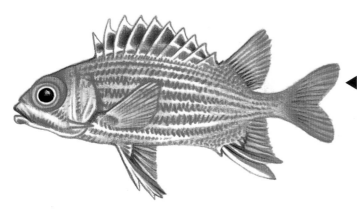

Sabre squirrelfish
Sargocentron spiniferum

Its body is moderately compressed and tall; the snout is pointed with relatively large eyes. The dorsal fin is well developed with red interradial membranes. Coloring of the body is red with spots of the same color, but darker on the opercula and at the base of the pectoral fins. This is a nocturnal species, and has territorial habits. It measures up to forty-five centimeters in length.

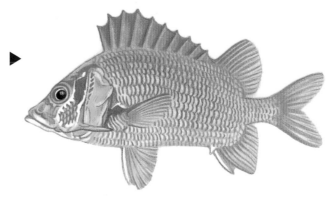

PLATYCEPHALIDAE FAMILY

Crocodile fish
Cociella crocodila

The body is compressed toward the front and is slightly cylindrical towards the rear; it is covered with rough scales. The mouth is large and is well lined with small, sharp teeth. There are two dorsal fins, the first of which is preceded by an isolated spine. The caudal fin is rounded. The coloring ranges from brownish to olive-gray, with dark spots on the back. Normally, it can be found on the seabed or partly buried in silt, by itself or in pairs. It grows to be sixty to seventy centimeters in length.

SCORPAENIDAE FAMILY

Clearfin turkeyfish
Pterois radiata

◄ Oblong body with a large head and a large mouth. The rays of the pectoral fins are very long, do not branch out, and the upper ones are joined by a membrane but only at the base. All of the rays are poisonous. The body is a brownish red with white stripes. Above the eyes there are long fleshy papillae. It can attain a size of twenty-five centimeters.

Lionfish
Pterois volitans

Body is similar to the previous species. The coloring presents broad brown vertical stripes; not all the same width. The rays of the fins are not naked, but possess a more or less developed membrane that makes them similar to feathers. The odd-numbered fins bear rows of brownish-black spots. Around the mouth and above the eyes one can clearly see some indented appendages. It can attain a size of thirtyf-ive centimeters.

Devil scorpionfish
Scorpaenopsis diabolus

◄ A slightly oval body, massive and high, with numerous fleshy excrescences. The head is large and is covered with spines; the mouth is wide and turns upwards. The pectoral fins extend to the anal fin. The coloring provides excellent camouflage, as this is a species that hunts from ambush. The tailfin has broad dark vertical stripes. The spines of the dorsal fin are poisonous, but not to the same degree as those of the stonefish. It grows to a length of thirty centimeters.

Stonefish
Synanceia verrucosa

A moderately oblong body, compressed at the sides and free of scales. The head is massive, covered with crests and spines, and the eyes - which are perhaps the most noticeable part - are turned upwards, as is the wide mouth. The pectoral fins are very well developed. The coloring provides excellent camouflage, and the fish is practically invisible because it is virtually identical to a stone. The glands at the base of the spines produce a very powerful poison, which can be fatal.

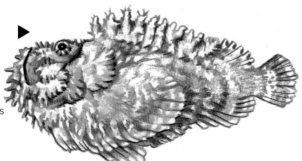

SERRANIDAE FAMILY

Scalefin anthias
Pseudanthias squamipinnis

◄ Oval, compressed body, which ends in a sickle-shaped tail with elongated lobes. The snout is short and rounded, and the mouth is terminal. The dorsal fin is well developed, especially in the male, which has several particularly long fore rays. The coloring is reddish, with red spots near the pectoral fins. The females have yellowish shadings. This fish is gregarious, and forms schools dominated by one or two males. They attain a length of fifteen to seventeen centimeters.

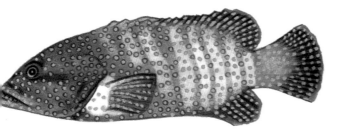

Peacock grouper
Cephalopholis argus

The body is massive, tapered, and slightly compressed. The head is powerful, with a slightly prominent lower jaw. The edge of the caudal fin is rounded. The dorsal fin has nine spinous rays and a rounded rear edge that ends in the proximity of the caudal peduncle and opposite the anal fin. The coloring is marked by numerous dark blue spots and by ten dark bands on the sides. The fins are dark blue. These fish attain a length of fifty centimeters.

Coral grouper
Cephalopholis miniata

The body is similar to that of *Cephalopholis argus*. The rear edges of the dorsal and anal fins are less rounded than in the previous species. The coloring is a very bright reddish-orange, with numerous small dark-blue ocellate spots scattered all over the body and fins, and tends to become darker in the adults. A fairly territorial species, it prefers to remain in the general vicinity of grottoes and underwater crannies. According to some observations, this fish tends to become gregarious during the mating season, and to gather to restrict areas. It attains a length of forty to forty-five centimeters.

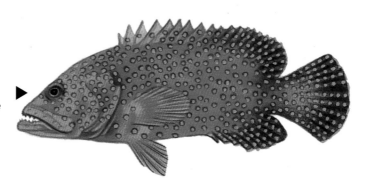

Lunartail grouper
Variola louti

Tapered body which terminates toward the rear with a tall caudal peduncle supporting an unmistakable tail in the form of a crescent moon or sickle, and with elongated lobes. Dorsal and anal fins have pointed rear edges. The coloring is reddish or brownish, with purple highlights and numerous pale spots. This is a fairly common species and attains lengths of up to eighty or eighty-five centimeters.

Potato cod
Epinephelus tukula

The body is broad and powerful. The head is tapered, with a convex intraorbital space. The snout is elongated and the mouth is wide. The lower jaw is more developed than the upper. The coloring is grayish-brown, with large, pronounced dark spots arrayed along the sides and on the tail. The fins are marked by smaller but numerous spots. This one is among the largest groupers, and can grow to be as long as two meters.

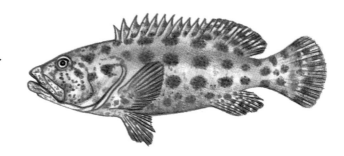

Giant grouper
Epinephelus tauvina

Tapered body, slightly compressed, but not as tall as other groupers. The snout is pointed, and the mouth is broad and terminal. The caudal fin is rounded. The dorsal fin is not very tall, and has eleven spinous rays. Along the back, at the base of the dorsal fin, it is possible to detect a number of large dark spots. Smaller spots are scattered along the entire body, whose coloring is basically very pale. This species can grow to be longer than two meters.

Redmouth grouper
Aethaloperca rogaa

Grouper with stout, tall, compressed shape. The head is large and the dorsal profile appears to be concave, in line with the eyes. The mouth is large and the lips are thick. Adults of this species have a sort of hump. The dorsal, anal, and caudal fins have a straight rear edge. The coloration is uniformly dark brown. The mouth and the opercula appear to be reddish. In the young of this species, the tail has a white edging. These fish live on other fish, and live along the reef. They grow to be sixty centimeters in length.

GRAMMISTIDAE FAMILY

Goldstriped goldfish
Grammistes sexlineatus

The body is oval, tall, and compressed, and is covered with many small scales. The mouth is wide, and the lower jaw bears a small fleshy excrescence. This species is easily recognized by its distinctive pattern of whitish-yellow stripes running lengthwise from the head to the caudal peduncle; these stripes are extremely noticeable on the dark brown and blue of the body. If this fish is alarmed, it secretes a mucus that is toxic to other fish. It grows to be thirty centimeters in length.

PSEUDOCHROMIDAE FAMILY

Sunrise dottyback
Pseudochromis flavivertex

The body is elongated, compressed, and is distinguished by a very long dorsal fin and a long anal fin. The eyes are in a subdorsal position and protrude slightly. The two-tone coloring is distinctive; it is a bright chrome yellow above, while the rest of the body is light blue. It lives by preference among the branches of coral, near a sandy bottom. This fish grows to be ten centimeters in length.

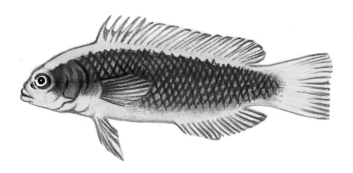

Olive dottyback
Pseudochromis fridmani

This species is only found in the Red Sea. The body is elongated and tapered toward the front. The snout is short, with large eyes and a terminal mouth. The caudal fin, which is truncated in the young, tends to have a slightly more elongated lower lobe in the adults of the species. This fish has a bright purple coloring, and is almost luminescent. A thin dark band runs from the tip of the snout to the eye. The opercula have a fairly pronounced dark blue spot. The upper lobe of the caudal fin is practically transparent. This species is often found under coral umbrellas that jut from the walls of the reef. They grow to be six to seven centimeters in length.

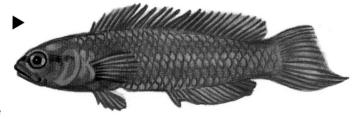

CIRRHITIDAE FAMILY

Longnose hawkfish
Oxycirrhites typus

The body is slightly cylindrical, taller at the center, and terminates in an elongated snout. The mouth is small. The spinous part of the dorsal fin bears a series of appendages. Pectoral fins are particularly well developed, and this fish uses them to balance upon gorgonians. Here the fish is perfectly camouflaged, due to a series of red stripes that form a checkerboard on its body. It attains a length of between ten and thirteen centimeters.

Goggle eye
Priacanthus hamrur

The body is oval, tall, and compressed. The snout is short, and the large eyes stand out, revealing the nocturnal habits of the species. The mouth is turned upward. The caudal fin is shaped like a crescent moon, with elongated lobes, especially in the adults of the species. The coloring is generally a dark reddish hue, but can change rapidly, acquiring more or less pronounced silvery highlights or becoming striped with red on silvery body. The dorsal and anal fins have dark highlights along their edges. This fish attains a length of forty to forty-five centimeters.

ECHENEIDAE FAMILY

Sharksucker
Echeneis naucrates

Elongated body with a head that is flattened dorsally, where the suction cup is found that is typical of remoras, and which is nothing more than a modified dorsal fin. The mouth features a well developed lower jaw. The dorsal and anal fins are similar and symmetrical. The coloring is dark gray or brownish with a darker band running lengthwise. The edges of the fins are whitish. This species attains a length of about a meter.

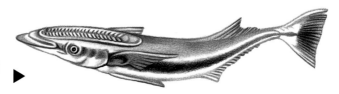

CARANGIDAE FAMILY

Bluefin Trevally
Caranx melampygus

The body is elongated, and rather tall; forward, it terminates with a convex head and a high forehead. The eyes are small. The caudal peduncle is narrow and reinforced with visible bony plates, the lateral line is complete and arched anteriorly. The coloring is greenish-brown, with numerous small black spots. The long, sickle-shaped pectoral fins with scales on their sides are yellow the young of the species. This fish grows to be longer than one meter.

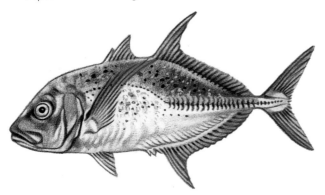

Bigeye Trevally
Caranx sexfasciatus

The body is elongated and compressed; the forward silhouette is rounded. The lower jaw tends to jut. On the caudal stalk, there are evident keels; the caudal fin is sharply forked. The coloring is blue-gray or blue-green on the back. The lobes of the caudal fin show a blackish hue. The sides are greenish-yellow or silvery. The young of the species are golden yellow, with four to seven broad dark vertical bands. This fish grows to be longer than a meter and a half.

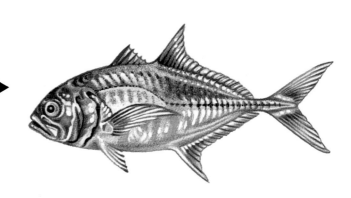

LETHRINIDAE FAMILY

Spangled emperor
Lethrinus nebulosus

The body is fairly tall and compressed. The head is elongated with a sharply oblique forward profile. The snout is pointed. The eyes tend upwards. The mouth is entirely red. The dorsal fin is well developed; the pectoral fins have scales on the inner section. The basic coloring, gray and uniform, is enlivened by light blue stripes and spots, more evident on the sides, on the opercula, and behind the eyes. Present in large numbers on open and shallow seabeds. It may measure seventy-five centimeters or more in length.

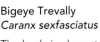

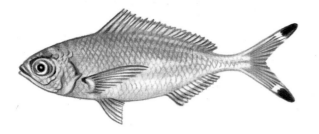

Suez fusilier
Caesio suevicus

The rounded and tapered body is rather elongated. The mouth is small and has thin teeth in front of a row of very small teeth. The upper jaw can be extended forward quite easily while capturing the small prey upon which the species feeds. Particularly distinctive is the forked caudal fin. The coloring is generally silvery, with yellow nuances; the lobes of the tailfin are black. These fish travel in numerous schools. They measure fifteen to twenty centimeters in length.

HAEMULIDAE FAMILY

Blackspotted grunt
Plectorhynchus gaterinus

The body is tapered, tall and slightly compressed. The head is well developed, the snout is short and convex. The eyes are large. The mouth is not very large and distinguished by a pair of thick lips. The adults are unmistakable, and have a basic coloring of bright yellow, upon which numerous black spots stand out. The young fish, instead, have five black longitudinal bands; the two bands closest to the back extend all the way back to the caudal fin. During daytime, this species tends to form schools close to the reef's slope. It measures up to fifty centimeters.

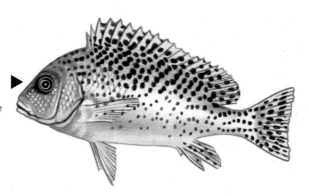

LUTJANIDAE FAMILY

Twinspot snapper
Lutjanus bohar

Elongated, tall, powerful body. The snout is pointed, and the mouth is wide and lined with one row of conical teeth above and below, and there are pronounced front canine teeth.
The fins are well developed. There is only one dorsal fin; the sickle-shaped pectoral fins stretch almost all the way to where the anal fin is attached. The coloring is a reddish-purple, darker on the back, and with yellowish highlights on either side of the head. The fins are dark, and are partly edged with white. The spinous rays of the dorsal fin are white at the tips. This fish attains a length of seventy to seventy-five centimeters.

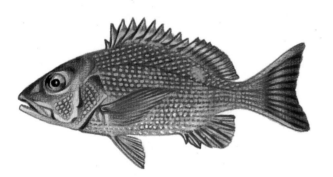

Bluestriped snapper
Lutjanus kasmira

Tapered body with pointed snout. Large eyes and mouth. The dorsal fin extends to the height of the caudal peduncle. The coloring is golden yellow on the back, becoming gradually paler along the sides and almost silvery on the belly. Typical of the species are the four light stripes running lengthwise; the longest of the stripes runs from the mouth to the caudal peduncle. The edges of the dorsal and the caudal fins are black. This fish measures forty centimeters in length.

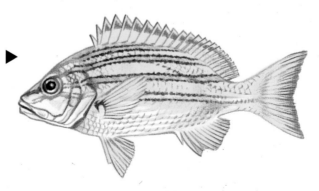

MULLIDAE FAMILY

Yellowsaddle goatfish
Parupeneus cyclostomus

The high, tapered body ends in a jutting snout. The lower jaw is distinguished by the presence of two long barbels that extend back to the ventral fins. The two dorsal fins are sharply separated. The tail is typically two-lobed. The head has bluish stripes that are fairly evident. The second dorsal fin has a dark spot toward the rear. The coloring is brighter in the young. It measures thirty-five centimeters in length.

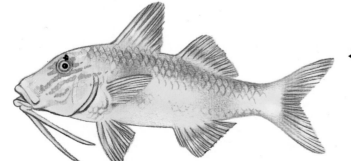

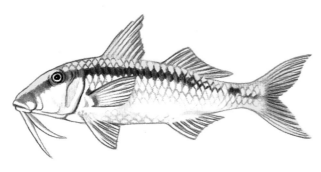

Forsskal's goatfish
Parupeneus forsskali

The shape of the body is typical of the genus *Parupeneus*. The barbels, which are still present, are however far smaller than those found in the previous species described. The coloring is a silvery blue with yellow nuances on the back. The caudal peduncle is bright yellow with a pronounced dark spot at the center. Along the sides there is a dark band which covers the eye. It measures thirty centimeters in length

PEMPHERIDAE FAMILY

Vanikoro sweeper (glassfish)
Pempheris vanicolensis

The body is oblong and compressed, taller toward the front and tapered toward the rear. The dorsal silhouette is nearly a straight line, while the ventral profile is concave around the long anal fin. The tail is slightly incised. The mouth is wide, oblique, and terminal. The eyes are large. This species is nocturnal, and forms numerous schools in the shelter of coral reefs. The coloring is light, pink and translucent. It measures twelve to fifteen centimeters in length.

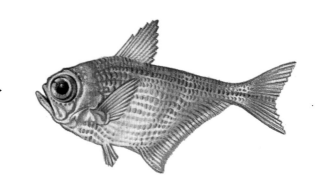

EPHIPPIDAE FAMILY

Batfish
Platax orbicularis

The unmistakably shaped body is tall, compressed, and discoid, with anal and dorsal fins that are symmetrical and well developed. Narrower in the young, these fins tend to broaden and become more rounded in adults. The mouth and the eyes are small. The coloring is distinguished by broad dark vertical bands along the sides, which tend to disappear with age. They live in schools. They measure fifty centimeters in length.

CHAETODONTIDAE FAMILY

Threadfin butterflyfish
Chaetodon auriga

The body is nearly rectangular, very tall and compressed. The head is concave toward the front, and terminates in a pointed, short snout. A broad dark band covers the eye, narrowing on the back. The dorsal fin features a dark ocellate spot along the rearmost edge, topped by a number of elongated and filamentous rays which constitute one of the distinctive features of this species. The Chaetodon auriga swims alone or in pairs. It measures twenty to twenty-five centimeters in length.

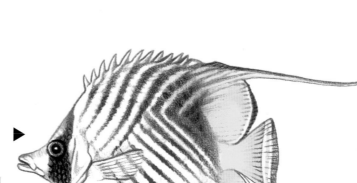

Exquisite butterflyfish
Chaetodon austriacus

The body is typically oval and compressed. The snout is short. The dorsal fin is very long. The anal fin is well developed. The rear edges of the fins just mentioned seem to shade into the caudal fin. The background coloring is yellow. Along the sides, there is a series of slightly diagonal stripes of a blue-black color. The snout is dark and a vertical black stripe entirely covers the eye. The anal fin, the caudal fin, and the rear edge of the dorsal fin are black. This species feeds entirely on polyps. This fish measures twelve centimeters in length.

Striped butterflyfish
Chaetodon fasciatus

The shape of the body is similar to that of *Chaetodon austriacus*. The background coloring is yellow. Along the sides, nine or ten slightly diagonal bands of a dark color stand out, and merge into a single band of the same color parallel to the dorsal fin. The dorsal, caudal, and anal fins are trimmed with a brownish-yellow band. The black eye band is followed by shorter white band. It measures eighteen centimeters in length.

Blackback butterflyfish
Chaetodon melannotus

The body appears nearly oval, tall and compressed. The head has an oblique and slightly concave forward profile. The snout is short and pointed. The most distinctive feature of this species is the black band that vertically cuts across the snout, covering the eye. The rear portion of the caudal peduncle and forward portion of the anal fin have black spots. All of the fins are yellow. On the sides of this fish there are diagonal rows of points that converge in a dark dorsal band. These fish attain a length of eighteen centimeters.

Paleface butterflyfish
Chaetodon mesoleucos

A slightly square body, extremely compressed laterally, and tall. The forward profile is convex. The snout is short. The forward portion is white and the rear portion is brown, with twelve black vertical stripes. The caudal fin is black and is trimmed in white, with a whitish, orange-tipped crescent. The upper silhouette of the snout is marked by a black band that covers the eyes. It measures fourteen to sixteen centimeters in length.

Crown butterflyfish
Chaetodon paucifasciatus

The body is tall and compressed. The snout is pointed. The background color is quite pale. The forward section is whitish with a strip of tawny reddish-yellow covering the eye. On the sides are four or five bands of black diamond shapes. On the rear part of the body there is a distinctive red spot. A band of red distinguishes the caudal fin. In young specimens, at the center of the red spot there is an ocellar dot. This fish generally swims in pairs or in small groups near the underwater meadows. It measures fourteen centimeters in length.

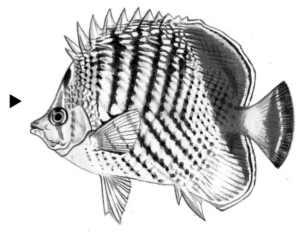

Masked butterflyfish
Chaetodon semilarvatus

◄ The species is peculiar to the Red Sea. The shape is almost discoid, with a small prominent snout. The colouring is almost uniformly orange-yellow with fine dark diagonal stripes.
The eye is surrounded by a dark bluish spot that extends as far as to the operculum. A dark narrow line underscores the outline of the dorsal and anal fins. The pectoral fins are transparent; the ventral fins are yellow. These fish are often found in schools. They grow to be eighteen to twenty centimeters in length.

Pennantfish
Heniochus intermedius

The body is tall, disk-shaped, and extremely compressed. The head is small, the snout is slightly elongated. The forward portion of the body is distinguished by a broad black band that covers the eye and the operculum and extends to the base of the dorsal fin. A second band runs diagonally along the rear portion of the body, starting from the caudal peduncle. The spinous ray of the dorsal fin is prominent as a banner. This fish measures twenty-five centimeters in length.

►

POMACANTHIDAE FAMILY

Emperor angelfish
Pomacanthus imperator

◄ The shape of the body is nearly oval, with a practically rectilinear forward profile of the head. The snout is very short. The dorsal and anal fins have a rounded forward edge that just exceeds the caudal stalk. The young of this species are dark blue with lighter concentric bands, the last of which forms a closed circle on the caudal stalk. Adults feature many diagonal yellow bands. The eyes are masked by a black stripe edged in light blue, followed by a similar stripe on the operculum. This fish grows to a length of thirty-five centimeters.

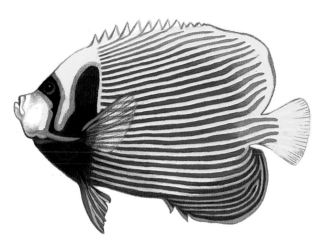

Arabian angelfish
Pomacanthus asfur

The body is tall and compressed. The head has a convex forward profile which ends in a short snout. The lower jaw is slightly prominent. The dorsal and anal fins are well developed, and their rays extend far backwards, way past the rear margin of the caudal fin. The coloring of the young, with vertical whitish-yellow stripes, becomes a uniform dark blue in adults, which can be distinguished by the yellow spot on the sides, which extends to part of the back and the tail in the same color. This fish has a length of thirty or thirty-five centimeters.

►

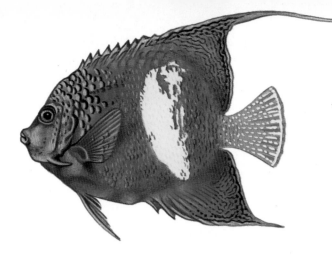

Yellowbar angelfish
Pomacanthus maculosus

The shape of the body is quite similar to that of *Pomacanthus asfur*. The young of the species have light vertical stripes on the sides, and can be distinguished from the young of *Pomacanthus asfur* because their caudal fins are light in color and translucent. The adult features a large yellow spot on their side, which however does not extend to the dorsal area of the base of the dorsal fin. These fish tend to be solitary, and grow to a length of thirty centimeters.

Royal angelfish
Pygoplites diacanthus

The body is less tall than usual in angelfish. The rear edges of the dorsal and anal fins are well developed, but do not exceed the caudal fin. The body has a background coloring of orange yellow, with eight or nine dark blue bands. The eyes are surrounded by two sharply defined dark blue stripes. The dorsal fin has a fairly dark vermiculation, while the anal fin has parallel yellow stripes along the edge of the fin. The young of this species are fairly similar, and have a posterior ocellar spot. This fish grows to a length of twenty-five or thirty centimeters.

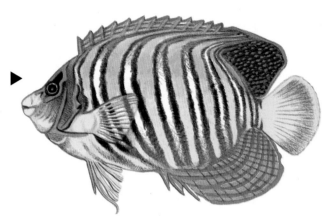

POMACENTRIDAE FAMILY

Sergeant major
Abudefduf saxatilis

Configuration of the body is similar to the other described species. The grayish silvery coloring shifts toward bright yellow on the back. Along the sides of the fish, there are five dark vertical bands, the first of which intersects the rearmost edge of the operculum. The coloring becomes lighter when the fish lives near sandy seabeds, and darker near coral. Adult males acquire bluish and purplish nuances when they are guarding the spawn. They attain a length of ten to fifteen centimeters.

Twobar anemonefish
Amphiprion bicinctus

The body is oval and rounded. The snout is short and stubby, with a small mouth. The dorsal fin extends along much of the dorsum and presents a slight saddle formation which separates the spinous portion from the part with soft rays. The caudal fin has two lobes. The background coloring ranges from orange to brownish orange, with two white vertical strips. The younger specimens may have a third stripe on the stalk of the tailfin. It generally tends to live in symbiosis with anemonefish of the genus *Heteractis*. It attains a length of thirteen to fifteen centimeters.

Bluegreen chromis
Chromis viridis

The shape of the body is roughly similar to the damselfish of the Mediterranean. The coloring tends to bluish, and is relatively intense, with slight nuances along the edge of the scales. This fish is gregarious, and tends to form large groups, each of which seems to colonize a specific coral formation, favoring those near the sheer walls at the outer edge of the reef. They measure from eight to ten centimeters in length.

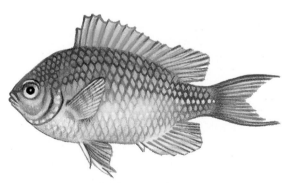

Banded dascyllus
Dascyllus aruanus

The body is fairly stubby, squarish, tall, and compressed. The mouth is small with a slightly prominent lower jaw. The background coloring is whitish, with three distinctive diagonal dark bands, the first of which covers the eye and the mouth. This fish forms small groups, each of which is closely associated with a single coral colony. Only larger specimens venture at any distance from the corals, while smaller ones remain in permanent residence among the branches. They measure eight to ten centimeters in length.

Half-and-half chromis
Chromis dimidiata

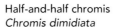

The shape of the body is similar to the species described immediately above. The coloring, however, is radically different, and allows one to recognize this species quite easily; half the body is white and half is dark brown or black. This fish is gregarious, and tends to form huge schools near large coral formations, venturing to greater depths than the *Chromis viridis*. It measures seven centimeters in length.

Domino damselfish
Dascyllus trimaculatus

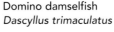

The shape of the body is typical of the genus. The mouth is small, considering that this is a fish feeding on plankton. The coloring is the most distinctive feature, and quite sufficient to make the fish unmistakable. In fact, this species is either completely black or dark brown, with three white spots: one on either side and a third on the forehead. These spots are most pronounced in the young, and tend to fade in adulthood. The species is quite common around anemonefish, amidst long-spined black urchins (*Diadema antillarum*), and amidst acropora corals. It measures up to fourteen centimeters in length.

LABRIDAE FAMILY

Yellowtail wrasse
Anampses meleagrides

Tapered body, with a generally oval silhouette, and with a slight frontal hump, more pronounced in females. The mouth is terminal, and protractile, with large fleshy lips. The coloring of adult males is dark and purplish with more-or-less elongated bluish spots along the edge of the scales. Dorsal and anal fins feature bluish stripes, as does the rearmost edge of the caudal fin, the lobes of which are elongated. Females have a dark coloring, spangled with numerous white spots. The snout and the lower head are reddish. The caudal fin is yellow. This fish measures up to twenty-five centimeters in length.

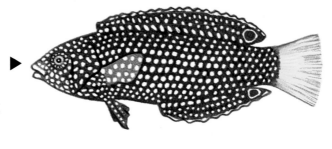

Abudjubbe wrasse
Cheilinus abudjubbe

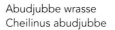

A member of the Labridae family with a particularly powerful structure, with a tall body covered with large scales. The head is elongated and convex; the mouth is well developed with pronounced canine-shaped teeth. The background coloring is dark, especially along the side, where a number of red spots can be seen. Distinctive red stripes are arrayed around the eyes. The fins are lighter in color and distinguished by yellow-greenish spots, distributed in rows along the rays. This fish often feeds on sea urchins. It measures thirty-five centimeters in length.

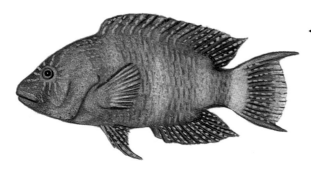

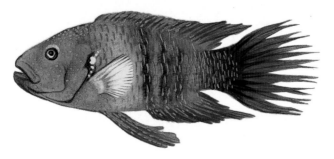

Broomtail wrasse
Cheilinus lunulatus

The body is compressed and tall, with large scales. The head is convex and stubby with a short tail. The mouth is large and protractile. Males have a relatively dark background coloring, especially on the head, and feature purple stripes that are sometimes particularly pronounced along the edges of the scales. The pectoral fins are yellow. Bluish nuances distinguish the mouth and fins. The caudal fin is distinguished by a fringed rear edge that is peculiar to the species. This fish measures up to fifty centimeters in length.

Humphead wrasse
Cheilinus undulatus

The humphead wrasse is the largest known member of the Labridae family, and has a very distinctive tall and stubby structure. The mouth is large and features thick protractile lips which allow this fish literally to suck up its prey. In the adults, the head is marked by a pronounced bump on the forehead. The greenish-gray coloring has irregular greenish-yellow stripes along the sides, shifting to orange on the head. These fish can be as long as two meters, and can weigh more than one hundred and seventy to one hundred and eighty kilograms.

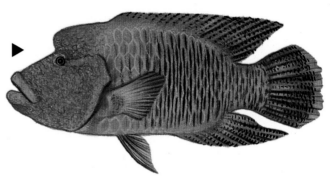

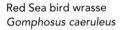

African coris
Coris africana

Tapered, slender body, with a silhouette reminding one of the Mediterranean rainbow wrasse. The first two rays on the dorsal fin are generally elongated, in adult specimens. The reddish coloring features fine greenish stripes at the base of each scale. The head is greenish and has broad greenish bands, the widest of which runs from the rear edge of the mouth to the operculum. Males have a green stripe along the side, just above the point of origin of the anal fin. This fish reaches a length of thirty-five to forty centimeters.

Red Sea bird wrasse
Gomphosus caeruleus

A typically oval body, slightly compressed. The snout is distinctively elongated and tubular in the adults. The mouth is terminal, but sufficiently well developed to prey on small animals. The caudal fin is rounded, but tends to develop elongated lobes with time. The coloring is dark blue in males. Females are green on their backs and yellowish on their bellies, with black spots on their sides. They measure from twenty to twenty-five centimeters in length.

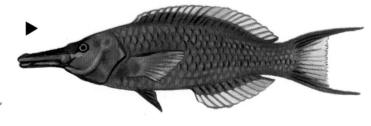

Cleaner wrasse
Labroides dimidiatus

The body is compressed, elongated, and covered with large scales. The head is pointy; the snout is elongated, with a small terminal mouth lined with numerous small and pointed teeth. The upper jaw is longer than the lower. The forward half of the body is brownish, and darker on the back than on the belly.
A broad black band runs from the beginning of the snout all the way to the tip of the caudal fin, widening as it goes. The base of the anal fin and the rear part of the body are an intense dark blue. It attains a length of ten centimeters.

Moon wrasse
Thalassoma lunare

The body is tapered, powerful, and slightly compressed. The head is rounded, the snout is short. The mouth is small and the lips are thin. The caudal fin is truncated in the young; partially moon-shaped in adults, especially larger males, which are also bluish. The coloring is greenish with vertical purplish-red stripes on the sides. The head is greenish-blue with broad pink bands running roughly lengthwise. The caudal fin is yellowish at the center with pink stripes along the lobes. It attains a length of twenty-five to thirty centimeters.

SCARIDAE FAMILY

Rusty parrotfish
Scarus ferrugineus

The body is tapered, slightly compressed at the sides, and covered with large scales. The head is large and the mouth is in a terminal position. The upper jaw is slightly prominent. One distinctive feature is the large teeth of the jaws, which join together so as to form a beak of four plates. The male, which has a greenish snout and fins edged in blue-green, is more colorful than the female. This fish prefers a protected coral seabed. It attains a length of forty centimeters.

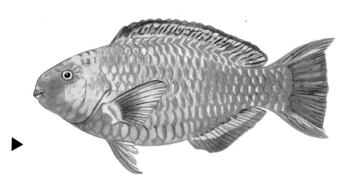

Steephead parrotfish
Scarus gibbus

The body is oval, tall, and powerful. The head has a forward silhouette that is quite convex, and nearly vertical. The dental plates are not particularly pronounced. On the cheeks, are three rows of large scales. The caudal fin is semilunar. The coloring is brownish yellow, while the lower part of the snout is green in the females. On the scales are fairly intense pink stripes. These remain in males as well; males have on their dorsal area a greenish coloring with touches of violet. The ventral section is blue-green. The rear of the caudal fin has a green edge. It attains a length of seventy centimeters.

Bumphead parrotfish
Bolbometopon muricatum

The body is powerful, tall compressed at the sides, and covered with large scales. At the sides of the snout and near the mouth there are three rows of scales. The coloring is greenish-blue both in males and females. The snout and the gullet are pink as is the forward portion of the prominence of the males, which can be thus easily recognized. The young of this species are dark brown, with a double row of white spots along the upper half of the body. They grow to be one and a half meters long.

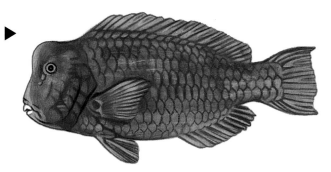

BLENNIIDAE FAMILY

Mimic blenny
Aspidontus taeniatus

The body is elongated and tapered. Its shape and coloring mimic the *Labroides dimidiatus*. Distinguishing between the two species is not simple, even for other fish, which are often thereby deceived by the mimic blenny. The most evidently distinguishing feature is the shape of the snout and of the mouth, which turn downward due to the greater development of the upper jaw. The black band running lengthwise is less developed. It measures twelve to thirteen centimeters.

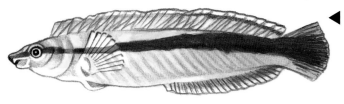

Blackfin barracuda
Sphyraena qenie

◀ The body is elongated and is typical of the barracuda. The lower jaw, devoid of any fleshy excrescence, is prominent, but the back of the jaw goes no further back than the forward margin of the eye. The first dorsal fin begins after the pectoral fins. The second dorsal fin is symmetrical with the anal fin. The caudal fin is forked, and strangely can have three lobes in the larger specimens. The coloring is silvery, with eighteen to twenty-two dark vertical bands. The dorsal and caudal fins are dark, as is the anal fin, while the last two anal rays are white. This species grows to over a meter in length.

GOBIIDAE FAMILY

Sixspot goby
Valenciennea sexguttata

The tapered body is covered with small rough scales; the snout is pointed and the mouth is turned slightly upward, lined with a great many teeth some of which are quite large. There are two dorsal fins; the first dorsal fin is marked by small round or oblong dark blue spots. Along this fish's sides are one or two barely visible stripes, which do not reach the caudal fin. It lives part of the time buried in sandy seabeds. This fish grows to a length of thirteen centimeters. ▶

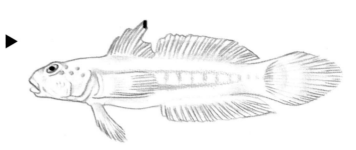

ACANTHURIDAE FAMILY

Black surgeonfish
Acanthurus gahham

The body is oval, tall and slightly compressed. The forward profile is rounded. The dorsal and anal fins are well developed. The ◀ caudal fin, distinguished by a white band at its base, is sickle-shaped, with the upper and lower lobes elongated. A short black band can be seen behind the eyes alongside the spines of the caudal peduncle. The pectoral fins have a dark yellow border. This fish grows to a length of forty centimeters.

Brown surgeonfish
Acanthurus nigrofuscus

The body is oval, tall and compressed. The forward profile is extremely convex. The snout is dark brown or purplish-brown, with or without thin bluish-gray lines running lengthwise along the side. The lips are black. The rear edges of the anal and dorsal fins are distinguished by a black spot. The head and chin have numerous orange spots. The spine on the peduncle is bordered in black. This fish grows to a length of twenty centimeters.

▶

Sohal surgeonfish
Acanthurus sohal

The body is oval, tall, and compressed. The head is powerful and rounded. The mouth is distinguished by thick lips and spatulate teeth suited to grazing on algae, on which this fish feeds. The ◀ coloring is bluish-gray, with numerous dark stripes along the side and the upper part of the head. The cheeks are white. The fins are dark and edged with a light-blue band. The fearsome spines on the caudal peduncle are distinguished by their bright orange color. This fish behaves in a territorial manner, and attains a length of forty centimeters.

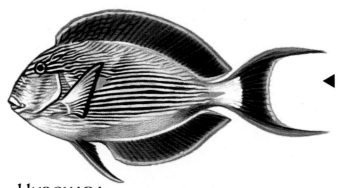

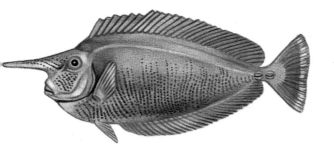

Spotted unicornfish
Naso brevirostris

This is the most distinctive of the surgeonfish, easily recognized for its powerful oval body that terminates in a long beak, which in turn extends well beyond the snout. On the sides of the peduncle there are two bony plates each one bearing a sharp spine. The caudal fin is rounded. The coloring ranges from grayish-blue to olive brown. The lips are sometimes bluish.
The tail features a pale band along the lower edge. This fish has gregarious habits, and attains a length of fifty centimeters.

Orangespine unicornfish
Naso lituratus

The body is oval, compressed, and tall toward the front. The head is powerful with a dorsal profile that forms a forty-five degree angle. The snout is pointed; the mouth is small and is lined with sharp teeth with rounded tips. On the sides of the peduncle are two bony plates, each bearing a sharp spine which curves forward. The caudal fin is semilunar, with pointed lobes and long filamentous rays. The coloring is yellowish-brown. The caudal peduncle is orange. Between the eyes is a light yellow spot. The dorsal fin is yellowish-orange, black at the base, with a white edge. This fish attains a length of forty-five centimeters.

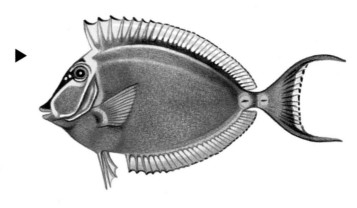

Bluespine unicornfish
Naso unicornis

The body is oval and elongate, tall and compressed. The forward profile is marked by a beak that is not long enough to exceed the mouth. The snout is pointed; the mouth is terminal, with powerful compressed teeth. On the sides of the caudal peduncle are two bluish spines shaped like chisels, which are not movable, but attached to bony plates. The coloring is light gray, and olive. In some cases the lips are blue and the dorsal and anal fins have orange stripes. The caudal fin is crescent-shaped with elongated, filmentous lobes. This fish attains a length of fifty to sixty centimeters.

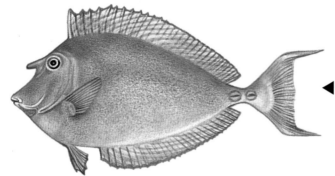

Yellowtail surgeonfish
Zebrasoma xanthurum

The body is compressed laterally and covered with small scales. The forward portion of the silhouette of the snout is typically concave. The mouth is small, terminal and protractile. The single dorsal fin is well developed, rounded to the rear, and almost symmetrical to the anal fin. The spines on the caudal peduncle can vary in size. The coloring is dark blue, with small reddish spots on the head, which tend to follow a straight-line array behind the eyes, ending at the pectoral fin. The caudal fin and the edge of the pectoral fins are bright yellow. This fish grows to a length of forty centimeters.

SIGANIDAE FAMILY

Stellate rabbitfish
Siganus stellatus

Oval, compressed body, covered with very small scales. The snout is slightly pointed; the mouth is terminal and is lined with numerous small teeth. The cheeks are covered with large scales. The coloring is generally a grayish-green spangled with small brown spots that tend to become smaller toward the back of the head, where they form a green oval shade at the base of the spines of the dorsal fin. Large black spots are present along the lateral line. This fish grows to a length of forty centimeters.

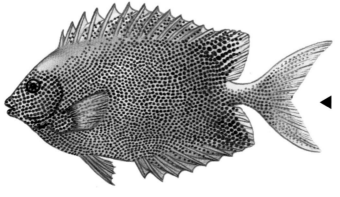

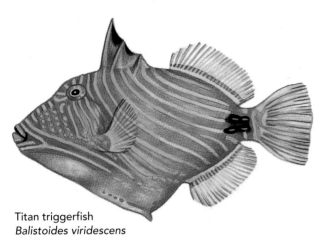

Titan triggerfish
Balistoides viridescens

The shape of the body is typical of the family. The mouth is terminal. There is a deep depression between the eyes. On the stalk of the caudal fin are two to four rows, running lengthwise, of large tubercles. The coloring is greenish; the edges of the fins are black. A black band runs around the upper jaw. The stalk of the caudal fin is fairly light in color. This species is aggressive, especially during the mating season. This fish grows to a length of seventy to seventy-five centimeters.

Orangestriped triggerfish
Balistapus undulatus

A slightly oval body, tall and compressed, covered with small bony plates. The head is very well developed and measures roughly a third of the length of the body. The eyes are quite far along the side of the fish. The mouth is terminal, and is distinguished by powerful jaws lined with massive teeth. The background coloring is dark, and orange-yellow stripes stand out on it. Bands of the same color surround the mouth. The dorsal and anal fins are light blue. The caudal fin is yellow. This fish grows to a length of seventy centimeters.

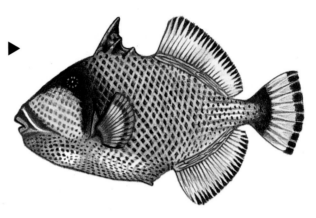

Redtooth triggerfish
Odonus niger

The body is slightly oval. The head is pointed. The mouth is terminal, and the lower jaw is more developed than the upper. The coloring of the body is blue-black while the head is greenish with bluish stripes leading from the mouth. The caudal fin is semilunar, and the lobes are well developed and quite long. This fish tends to gather in small groups, and grows to a length of fifty centimeters.

Blue yellow spotted triggerfish
Pseudobalistes fuscus

The shape of the body is typical of the family. The head is rounded. There are large scales under the opercula. Along the lower portion of the snout there are horizontal channels. The coloring is dark brown with yellow or orange spots on the scales. The edge of the fins is yellowish. The caudal fin is rounded in the young and has elongated lobes in adults. This fish grows to a length of fifty to fifty-five centimeters.

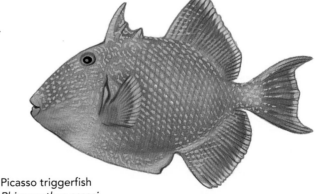

Picasso triggerfish
Rhinecanthus assasi

The body is oval and the head triangular, the snout is pointed and the mouth is terminal. On the stalk of the caudal fin, there are three rows of small spines. The lips are yellowish and a stripe of the same color extends from the mouth to the operculum. A black vertical band covers the eyes. On the sides are diagonal stripes. The caudal fin is slightly rounded. This fish grows to a length of twenty-five to thirty centimeters.

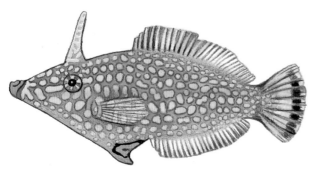

OSTRACIIDAE FAMILY

Cube boxfish
Ostracion cubicus

The body is shaped like a box, rectangular with rounded off angles and corners, and has no spines. The dorsal and anal fins are small, but are driven by powerful muscles which the fish uses for locomotion. The ventral and caudal fins are more developed; the caudal serves as a rudder. Males have a uniform violet coloring. The young of the species are yellow with black spots. This fish grows to a length of forty-five centimeters.

MONACANTHIDAE FAMILY

Harlequin filefish
Oxymonacanthus halli

The body is oval and compressed, and is covered with a rough epidermis, due to the presence of minuscule denticles. The snout is typically elongated and tubular, with a lower jaw that is more developed than the upper. The background coloring is green, with a regular pattern of large bright yellow or orange spots. It forms small groups near branches of Acropora corals, on the polyps of which it feeds. This fish grows to a length of ten or twelve centimeters.

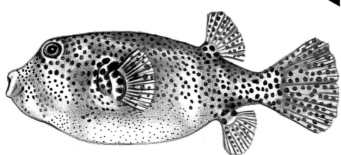

Pearl toby pufferfish
Canthigaster margaritata

This is a blowfish with slightly compressed head and body dotted with small spines which become pronounced when the fish swells up. The snout is elongated and the mouth is protractile. The caudal fin is truncated. At the center of the back and the belly there is a fold of skin which can be erected.
The coloring is dark yellow on the back, and shades off on the belly. The body is dotted with dark blue spots edged in black. Around the eyes there are radial stripes, of the same color as the ocellar spots. At the base of the dorsal fin, are two dark blue stripes. This fish grows to a length of twelve or thirteen centimeters.

TETRADONTIDAE FAMILY

Blackspotted pufferfish
Arothron stellatus

The body is elongated and globular, with an oval silhouette, and is covered with small spines. The young of the species have a rubbery texture, while adults are more flaccid. The mouth is powerful and equipped with two large adjacent dental plates on each jaw. The coloring is typically mottled.
In the young, the belly is marked by pronounced black stripes. The base of the pectoral fins is black. This fish propels itself along with its dorsal and anal fins. It is common to encounter this species on the sandy bottoms of lagoons. It grows to a length of one hundred to one hundred and twenty centimeters.

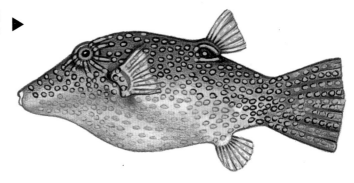

DIODONTIDAE FAMILY

Burrfish
Diodon hystrix

Tapered body, rounded toward the front, with large sharp spines which generally have split bases. These spines stand erect when the animal puffs up. The mouth has a single dental plate for each jaw. The snout and tail are elongated. The brownish-yellow coloring is fairly dark, with numerous black spots on the sides and the back. Nocturnal by habit, it seeks out sheltered places during the day. It is common, and in certain areas a diver may encounter dozens in a single dive. This fish grows to a length of ninety centimeters.

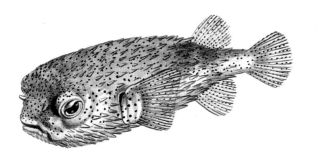

168 - The pixy hawkfish (Cirrhitichthys oxycephalus), which is up to 10 cm long, is almost always motionless among the corals or on the branches of gorgonians, where it waits for small prey to pass.

ACKNOWLEDGMENTS

Thanks to the following who helped make this book possible:
Diving World Hurghada for its willingness to provide all information necessary on the diving sites at Hurghada and Gobal.
Diving TGI El Gouna and Scuba Services Quseir for giving us invaluable details on diving sites near El Gouna and Quseir.
Special thanks to **Gigi Ferrari** of Diving World Hurghada, who with his in-depth knowledge of the entire area patiently helped us lay out the details of each dive."

PHOTOGRAPHIC CREDITS

All the photographs in this guide were provided by Massimo Bicciato and Giorgio Mesturini except the following:
NASA: pages 6A and 7B.